© 1995 Royal Smeets Offset bv
All rights reserved

Editions of this book will appear simultaneously in France, Great Britain, Italy and the Netherlands
under the auspices of Euredition bv, Den Haag, Netherlands

This edition published by Magna Books, Magna Road, Wigston, Leicester LE18 4ZH, England

ISBN 1 85422 873 0

Translation: Tony Langham
Typesetting: Zspiegel grafische zetterij, Best
Printed in The Netherlands by Royal Smeets Offset, Weert

Production: VBI/SMEETS
Compilation: BoekBeeld, Utrecht
Design and text of plan, planting plan, flowering and colour scheme: Bureau Willemien Dijkshoorn BNT,
Amsterdam
Editor A-Z: Yvonne Taverne, Utrecht
Editor-in-chief: Suzette E. Stumpel-Rienks, Bennekom
Photographs: Plant Pictures World Wide, Haarlem
Trade Photographs: Vaste Keurings Commissie, Aalsmeer
Planning and maintenance, text: Suzette E. Stumpel-Rienks, Bennekom;
Drawings: Theo Schildkamp, Haaksbergen
Small workers in the garden, text and drawings: Theo Schildkamp, Haaksbergen

This edition has been compiled with the greatest possible care. Neither the compiler nor the editor
accepts any liability for any damage as a result of possible inaccuracies and/or omissions in this
edition.

Flowering Houseplants

Flowers & Plants

MAGNA BOOKS

Contents

Index

Introduction

Enhancing the home

Plants have been cultivated for centuries, both for their practical uses and their ornamental value. Initially, this was done mainly in botanical gardens, to satisfy people's curiosity about new and unfamiliar plants. Gradually, plants were brought indoors as decoration, and commercial cultivation began. So the concept of a houseplant is not a botanical one; rather it was introduced by commercial growers.

Over the course of time, a process of selection has taken place, often involving exotic plants which can successfully be used in the microclimate of an indoor environment. There is a very wide range of such plants available, usually year-round.

It is essential to provide the right balance of light, air and soil humidity, and temperature if indoor plants are to remain healthy. When you choose them, it is important to give some thought to where in the house they will be positioned, and how much care and attention they will need.

Houseplants can broadly be divided into two groups:
– flowering plants, whose main ornamental value lies in their flowers;
– foliage plants, grown mainly for their leaves and growth habit.

Obviously there are many sub-groups within each of these divisions: ferns, bulbous and tuberous plants, cacti, trailing and climbing plants and so on. Some of these are dealt with in separate volumes.

This book deals with flowering houseplants, which can be divided into those which flower once and are then usually thrown on the compost heap, and those which will go on growing and flowering year after year if properly looked after.

Plants which flower once are often grown in groups of one colour in a trough or window box, with their often bright colours making an attractive focal point to a room. After these have flowered, they are less easy on the eye and usually not worth keeping.

The more long-lasting flowering houseplants need regular care in the form of watering, feeding and repotting. A combination of several different plants can affect both the microclimate and the appearance of a room, providing added humidity and, to a limited extent, removing unwanted substances from the air.

An attractive combination of well-chosen plants and containers can serve as a pleasant everyday reminder of the beauties of nature.

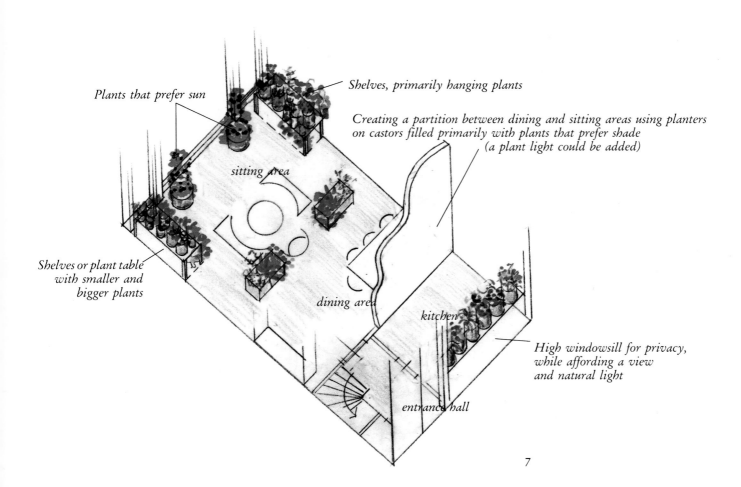

Plants that prefer sun

Shelves, primarily hanging plants

Creating a partition between dining and sitting areas using planters on castors filled primarily with plants that prefer shade (a plant light could be added)

sitting area

Shelves or plant table with smaller and bigger plants

dining area

kitchen

entrance hall

High windowsill for privacy, while affording a view and natural light

The design

Plan

The houseplants in this home have been chosen to make the maximum use of the limited amount of space available. Plants are an important part of the furnishings, but they need to be grown in suitable positions. Where they are placed will depend on the different purposes the rooms are used for, how many people live in the home, whether space is needed for children and pets, and of course cleaning requirements.

A certain amount of discipline is needed when choosing houseplants; otherwise, the result can all too easily be a jumble of bright colours.

This design creates clear dividing lines between the different functions of a room, such as seating and dining areas. It also uses symmetry to create a sense of calm and order.

On either side of the seating area, flowering plants are arranged on tables; rows of plants on shelves can also look very good. These are placed close to the window for maximum light, though most plants can be damaged by too much direct sunlight and may need protection in the form of net curtains or a movable screen.

The smaller plants forming the dividing line with the dining area can be placed on tables of varying heights, perhaps with castors so that they can be moved around to make extra space when necessary.

The two pots by the back doors are also on wheeled trolleys, which means that they do not need dishes underneath to hold water. These pots can also be taken outdoors in summer if required.

Kitchens, like bathrooms, are very good places for plants because they tend to have a high level of humidity.

In this particular plan, the kitchen window only gets sunlight at the end of the day, and is therefore an ideal place for houseplants, with plenty of light and humidity, but almost no direct sunlight.

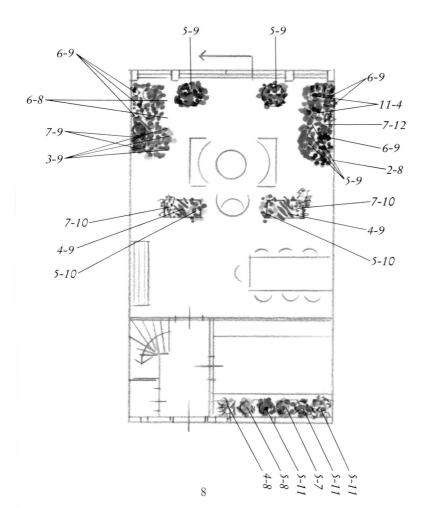

Month of flowering period

Planting plan

Most houseplants originate in tropical or subtropical regions, and require more or less constant warmth and humidity. Many rooms provide plenty of heat, but not nearly enough humidity, and the plants will therefore need a little extra assistance if they are to grow successfully.

Growers are able to simulate the proper growing conditions in a greenhouse; this is also possible in a house, where plants will need a careful combination of light, temperature, watering and feeding. But houses do not naturally provide sufficient humidity, because plants and humans have different requirements in this respect.

The "island" method involves standing the plant in a bowl of water, which is kept constantly fresh, with the container slightly raised so that the root ball is not wet all the time. Damp moss can also be used for this purpose, either by growing it on the surface of the soil or placing moss-covered sticks into the soil.

Placing plants close together can also help to produce a humid atmosphere by creating a canopy of leaves which holds in the water vapour. Having the plants close together also makes it easier to spray them with water, but do not spray the flowers themselves. And never place plants in draughts: plants are much more sensitive to them than we are.

Some plants with brightly-coloured leaves, such as *Calathea*, need high levels of temperature and humidity which are not feasible in an indoor environment, and these are unlikely to last more than a few months. Plants with variegated leaves need more light because they contain less chlorophyll; if they are not given sufficient light, they will grow new leaves containing more chlorophyll, and will lose some or all of their variegation.

The planting plan takes all the above factors into account wherever possible. It does not include plants which flower only once, as some of these are an acquired taste and have a limited shelf life.

Most plants will appreciate repotting once a year, and this has also been borne in mind in the design. Plants in larger pots will go for a few years without repotting. The *Bougainvillea* in the two big posts by the window have been grown up columnar supports. Repotting is a very good opportunity to move the plants around on the tables or shelves.

The plant groups in the troughs all have similar growing requirements.

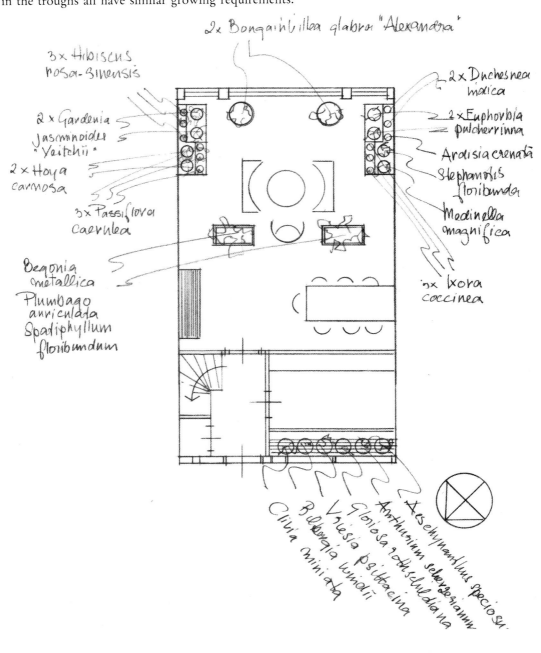

2x Bougainvillea glabra "Alexandra"

3x Hibiscus rosa-sinensis

2x Gardenia jasminoides "Veitchii"

2x Hoya carnosa

3x Passiflora caerulea

Begonia metallica
Plumbago auriculata
Spatiphyllum floribundum

2x Duchesnea indica

2x Euphorbia pulcherrima

Ardisia crenata

Stephanotis floribunda

Medinilla magnifica

3x Ixora coccinea

Aeschynanthus speciosus
Anthurium scherzerianum
Gloriosa rothschildiana
Vriesia psittacina
Beloperone guttata
Clivia miniata

Acalypha
Red-hot catstail

⚘ | 50-75 ○ ⊛ 5-9 🪴 ✂

Acalypha, originally indigenous in the islands of the Australian archipelago, is found growing wild throughout the tropics. It has a striking inflorescence, consisting of long, hanging, usually purplish-red tassels, although there are also species which are cultivated mainly for their coloured leaves, such as *A. wilkesiana*, which has bronze-green, yellow or red spotted leaves. This is a bushy plant with long-stemmed, bronze-green, oval, pointed leaves with serrated margins; the elegant cylindrical tassels, up to 50 cm long, grow from the axilla of the leaf stalks.
A. hispaniolae "Bode's Feuerzauber" (syn. *A. pendula*) has limp hanging branches and huge numbers of short red tassels; it is a good hanging plant. *A. hispida* has erect, branching or unbranched stems, and long hanging, red or purplish-red tassels which are slightly shorter in branching plants; "Alba" has yellowish-white tassels.
This plant thrives in very light spots, out of direct sunlight; always keep the soil moist, e.g., a mixture of leaf-mould or peat, sharp sand, old cow manure and some loam; water liberally with tepid water, spray and keep warm during the growing period (May to September, 16-20° C), and feed every two weeks. Slightly cooler and drier in winter (13-18° C). For fuller growth, pinch out growing tips (several times). Repot in spring. Propagate from cuttings in spring. Sensitive to red spider mite when humidity is too low.

Acalypha hispida pendula,
Red-hot catstail

Achimenes

⌂ ↕ 15-60 ⊘ ✿ 5-9 ⊡ ◁

The name *Achimenes* is derived from the Greek words, "a" (not, against) and "cheimon" (cold). It is indigenous in the tropical regions of Central and South America and certainly is not resistant to cold. Cultivars flower profusely as house plants.

This is a herbaceous, often hairy, bushy plant with caterpillar-shaped, scaly rootstocks ("tubers"), erect stems which do not branch out much, and dark green, oval to lanceolate, serrated leaves. There are five white, red, pink to purple or yellow flowers which end in a tube of fused petals. Each bloom lasts for 2-5 weeks.

A. erecta, 45 cm tall, has soft, hairy leaves, reddish stems, and numerous bright red blooms; *A. longiflora* has purplish-blue blooms with a white or red tube-shaped corolla, up to 6 cm long. It gave rise to many hybrids, including *Achimenes* "Little Beauty", with small pink blooms, "Paul Arnold", which has large purple blooms, "Rose", which has pink blooms, "Schneewittchen", which has bright white blooms, "Violet Charm", which has violet blooms, "Wijnrood", which has dark red blooms. *A. patens*, up to 15 cm tall, has brownish-green stems, serrated leaves and violet blooms.

This plant requires a light, warm, draught-free spot, out of direct sunlight, and lime-free, slightly acid soil, rich in humus, e.g., equal parts of leaf-mould, peat, sharp sand and some cow manure. Water regularly with tepid water (cold water on the leaves produces spots). Add some plant food to the water every two weeks. 20-30° C. The plant dies off above the ground after flowering (September). Cut stems and keep the clump dry over the winter at 15° C in January/February. Replant at a depth of 1-2 cm in fresh soil, keep moist at all times, 18-20° C. Propagate by dividing plant, from cuttings and seed (in this case, hybrids do not retain their shape). Spray frequently to avoid red spider mite.

Achimenes Rosa

left: Achimenes "Violet Charm"
below: Achimenes "Schneewittchen"

Aechmea

⬍ 40-60 ◉ ❀ 5-10 🪣 ◁

Most *Aechmea* species are epiphytic plants (they grow on trees without extracting nutrients from them) and they are mainly indigenous in the tropical rainforests of Brazil.

The long leaves grow in rosettes in a spiral, forming a dense cylinder at the base which always collects water. The growth of the rosette, which can take several years, concludes with a flower bud. The stem protrudes above the leaves, often with striking bracts. After flowering for a long time, the plant gradually dies down, but with some care it is possible to grow a new

flowering plant from the young rosettes on the parent plant. Using growth regulators, flowering plants are now available throughout the year.

A. chantinii has dark green, spiny leaves, 40 cm long, with white transverse stripes, and a bright orangey-red and yellow inflorescence. *A. fasciatia* has saw-edged, dark green leaves, up to 50 cm long, with numerous silvery stripes or spots; at the end of the stem there are spiny, pointed pink bracts and blue flowers. *A. fulgens* has greyish-green, saw-edged leaves, 50-60 cm long, reddish stems, no striking bracts, and beautiful red clusters of flowers; *A. fulgens* "Discolor" has leaves which are olive-green on the upper side and violet-red on the underside.

During the period of growth the plant requires a light spot protected from direct

Aechmea fasciatia

sunlight, and airy, well-drained soil, e.g., a mixture of leaf-mould, fern root and sphagnum moss. Minimum, 18° C. Water regularly with tepid, lime-free water. Add plant food (half concentration) to the water in the cylinder, once every two weeks. Spray in warm weather. In winter, minimum 15° C, less water, no plant food. When the plant is flowering, it can be placed in a darker spot. Propagate by removing young rosettes when they are half the height of the parent plant and have rooted.

Aeschynanthus
Basket vine

○ ↕ 50-300 ◐ ✿ 5-10 ⬚ ⊰

Aeschynanthus is mainly indigenous in the tropical rainforests of Southern Asia, and comprises more than 80 species, most of which are epiphytic plants. This plant has hanging or climbing stems, fleshy leaves in regular whorls, and attractive red flowers often arranged in groups at the end of the leaf stalks or in the leaf axilla.
A. lobbianus (syn. *A. radicans*), the lipstick vine, has rather woody, hanging stems up to 3 m long, shiny, leathery, lanceolate, dark green leaves, and numerous tubular, orangey-red flowers. When buying the plant, the buds should not be too developed to prevent them dropping off. *A. marmoratus* is a sturdy hanging plant with lanceolate leaves which are light-green with dark green veins on the upper side, and purple on the underside, with small, less striking scarlet flowers with a yellow calyx. *A. hildebrandii* and *A. speciosus* are more erect and have orange flowers.
This plant requires a bright spot, protected from direct sunlight, and acid, well-drained soil, e.g., a mixture of leaf-mould, sphagnum moss and sharp sand. Water generously and spray regularly for high humidity. During the flowering period, 17-20° C, and feed with plant food poor in nitrogen and lime once a week. Keep slightly cooler in winter (15° C) with less water, but keep soil moist. Repot in spring. Prune back *A. speciosus* to 2-3 pairs of leaves. Propagate from cuttings (spring).

Aeschynanthus lobbianus,
Basket vine

Aeschynanthus,
Basket vine

13

Anigozanthos

Anigozanthos

○ | 50-150 ○ ✿ 5-8 ! ▽

Anigozanthos means "plant with an unusual flower", and this is appropriate. This plant is indigenous in the subtropical areas of Australia. It has grass-like, sword-shaped leaves, and long, hairy, red or green stems with hairy, tube-shaped, yellowish-green or reddish-brown flowers, 4-8 cm long, which grow at the top in clusters. When they open, they curl upwards like the toes of a kangaroo.

A. flavidus has 100-175 cm long hairy, reddish-green stems, and yellowish-green to reddish-brown flowers. It is sometimes sold as cut flowers, as is A. manglesii, which has flowers with red petals and a green fringe; A. manglesii "Mini Prolific" is sold as a pot plant. Hybrids which are on the market often have the short-stemmed A. humilis as a parent plant.

This plant requires a light spot, plenty of fresh air, a large pot and well-drained soil. Always kept moist, e.g., equal parts of peat, coarse sand and loam. Water regularly. The plant can be placed outside in summer. Feed every two weeks. 16-30° C. Cooler in winter (5-15° C), and water less. Remove shoots when they have finished flowering. Repot after flowering. Propagate by dividing plant (spring).

Anigozanthos flavidus

Anthurium
Flamingo flower

○ │↕ 30-60 ⊘ ❀ 5-10 ! ⊔ ◁

Anthurium is indigenous in tropical rainforests in Central and South America, and it is usually the hybrids of *A. andreanum* and *A. scherzerianum* which are sold as house plants. They are cultivated both for their leaves and for their flowers. As a result of in vitro cultivation, a number of varieties are available throughout the year. The plant has dark green, leathery or velvety, coloured, heart-shaped or lanceolate leaves, often strikingly coloured bracts and straight or curved "palettes".

A. andreanum, the oil cloth flower, has short stems, many aerial roots (do not remove), and large shiny, heart-shaped, veined leaves up to 40 cm long with long stalks, and large, leathery, heart-shaped, coarsely veined, red, white, pink or salmon-coloured flower palettes, with a fairly thick, straight, cream-coloured flowering tail which curves slightly forwards. There are many hybrids with a large number of bigger, bright-coloured leaf bases. *A. scherzerianum* has virtually stalkless, broad, lanceolate leathery, dark green leaves up to 20 cm long, with a slightly lighter central vein and stems of the same length with shiny, round or oval bracts, which are usually red or sometimes red with white dots, salmon-coloured or greenish-white, and a curved or spiralling orange palette.

This plant requires a spot protected from direct sunlight and moist, well-drained soil. There is special soil available for *Anthuriums*. During the growing period, water frequently with soft water (to prevent spots on the leaves and flowers), spray and place plant on an upturned saucer in a dish of water. 20° C. Feed once a week with lime-free plant food (half concentration). For profuse flowering, keep the plant drier and cooler (15° C) in winter for 6-8 weeks. Repot in spring every two to three years. Propagate by dividing plants, removing side shoots which have taken root, and from stem cuttings of plants which have become ugly (spring).

Anthurium scherzerianum, Flamingo flower

Aphelandra
Zebra plant

○ ↕ 30-50 ⊘ ✿ 4-8 ▭ ✂

Aphelandra is indigenous in tropical and subtropical areas of America. It comprises about 300 species with red, orange and yellow flowers. Not many species are cultivated; *A. squarrosa* is the most important house plant.

A. squarrosa has broad, pointed, shiny, dark green leaves, up to 30 cm long, with prominent white markings, yellow blooms, consisting of large, overlapping bracts and smaller flowers with a calyx in five parts and two-lipped yellow, orange or red blooms. The cultivars with a yellow bloom are usually hybrids of the varieties, *Leopoldii* with red stems and splendid veined leaves, and *Louisae*, which also has beautifully veined leaves. *A. squarrosa* "Diana" grows as an attractive, compact plant with coarser markings; "Silver Queen" has more delicate light markings.

This plant needs a warm light spot protected against direct sunlight, and airy, nutritious soil, e.g., *Anthurium* potting compost, or potting compost with extra peat. Keep moist at all times. Water generously during the flowering period. Spray and wipe leaves with tepid, soft water. Give extra plant food every week, 18-25° C. Cooler in winter (10-14° C), and keep drier. Brown leaves mean that it is too cold or there is too much direct sunlight. If the soil is too dry, this encourages aphids. Remove flowerheads when flowering has finished. The plants can be topped or pruned. Repot in March. Propagate from (eye) cuttings (November to April).

Aphelandra squarrosa hybrid, Zebra plant

Ardisia
Coral berry

🌿 ↕ 50-100 ◷ ❀ 3-6 ✤ 9-5 🪣 ◁

Ardisia is indigenous in tropical woodland regions of southern and eastern Asia. It can bear beautiful shiny red berries for months on end. The thickened margins of the leaves contain the bacteria, *Bacillus follicola*, which are harmless to man. The plant lives in symbiosis with these bacteria and cannot survive without them. Without the bacillus, it inevitably dies.

This is an evergreen shrub with berries and spreading, dark green leaves, frizzy leaf margins, round berries, and pink or white fragrant flowers in the axilla or on the leaf stalks.

A. crenata (syn. *A. crispa*) has spreading twigs, leathery, shiny, dark green oval leaves, up to 10 cm long, large numbers of red berries which often remain on the plant for a long time, and fragrant, hanging, whitish-pink flowers; *A. crenata* "Alba" has white berries; "Albomarginata" has coloured leaves and red berries.

Place in a cool, airy, light spot, out of direct sunlight; good, moist potting compost; maximum, 22° C. Water regularly and spray (not during the flowering period). Give additional plant food every two weeks. Winter, 12-16° C (if it is warmer, the berries drop off), less water. Dust leaves; promote formation of berries by distributing pollen over the flowers with a brush. Repot in spring; for good, bushy growth, prune back to 5 cm. Propagate from cuttings and by sowing seeds. Sensitive to insecticides (aerosols).

Ardisia crenata, Coral berry

17

Begonia

• 🌢 ↕ 30-50 ⊘ ◉ ❀ all year round ⊔ ✂

Begonia comprises about 1,000 species which are indigenous in localized areas in tropical and subtropical regions in Africa, America and Asia, but are also found in the Andes and Himalayas. A number are suitable for placing in the windowsill; these are usually hybrids, which can be subdivided into single, semi-double and double varieties. This is a plant with a great diversity of heights, erect or hanging growth, size and colour of flower and leaf. Important parent plants of indoor begonias include *B. dregei*, 70-80 cm tall, with red, fleshy stems, bronze-green, irregularly serrated leaves with purple veins, and white clusters of flowers; *B. semperflorens*, 40 cm tall, a bushy plant with small, fleshy, shiny green or dark red oval leaves and white or red flowers, and *B. socotrana*, which has fresh green leaf stalks with bulbils in the axilla, shield-shaped, bright green leaves, indented in a funnel at the stalk, and dark pink clusters of flowers in winter.

B. albo-picta "Rosea" has short leaf stalks, narrow green leaves with silvery spots, and hanging pink clusters of flowers.

B. elatior hybrids (crossed from a parent plant such as *B. socotrana*) has countless cultivars with flowers in many colours, such as white, yellow, orange, pink or red, single or double. It flowers both in winter and in other seasons, but is difficult to keep after flowering. Single varieties include "Hoblanche", white flowers; "Schwabenland Rood", "Schwabenland Rose" and "Schwabenland Wit", large flowers; "Talia", red; "Yellow Melodie", large yellow. Semi-double varieties include "Arosa", dark pink; "Clara", white; "Ilona", yellowish-pink; "Netja", pink. Double varieties include "Alma", red; "Anja" and "Anne", yellow; "Barbara", pinkish-red, "Christine", pink and white; "Lone", old pink; "Orania", orange; "Paloma", white; "Rosanna", pink; "Sandra", white with a pink glow; "Susi", large pinkish-white. Propagate from top cuttings (winter) and shoots (summer).

B. "Gloire de Lorraine" hybrids (crossed from parent plants *B. dregei* and *B. socotrana*), (hanging) plants which flower in winter with small blooms; after flowering profusely once, it is difficult to keep the plant; limp stems, (dark) green, sometimes slightly marbled leaves, pink or white clusters of flowers (e.g., "Snow Princess"). Sensitive to mildew, do not keep the plant too moist. Propagate from leaf cuttings.

B. semperflorens hybrids are bushy plants up

top: *Begonia hybrid "Rosalie"*
bottom: *Begonia elatior hybrid "Aida"*

*Begonia elatior hybrid
"Paloma"*

Begonia Lorraine

to 40 cm tall, with small, fleshy, shiny, green or brown oval leaves, and large numbers of red, pink or white flowers in summer. They do tolerate sunlight. Propagate from seed, double varieties from cuttings. These plants require a light, draught-free spot protected against direct sunlight, and light, porous soil, rich in humus, e.g., potting compost, sharp sand, peat, and some rotted cow manure. During the growing period, water regularly with soft, tepid water. The soil should not dry out or be too wet (root rot). Do not spray leaves and flowers (attracts mildew). During the growing and flowering period, feed with plant food poor in lime (half concentration). Winter-flowering plants, maximum 18-20° C , otherwise they flower too quickly. After flowering, they are usually thrown away. Begonias which rest in winter should be placed in a cooler spot (15° C), less water. If the plants wilt, this means that there is too little light. Ugly, spotted leaves means that it is too warm. If flowers fall prematurely, the air is too dry. Repot in April. Propagate from cuttings and seed.

Beloperone
Shrimp plant

🌿 ↕ 40-90 ◯ ⬤ ✳ 4-9 🪣 ✂

Beloperone is indigenous in Mexico. It comprises about 60 species of tropical (semi-)shrubs, of which only *B. guttata* is available as a house plant.

B. guttata has hairy green stems up to 60 cm long, hairy, oval, bright green leaves, and striking, hanging flowerheads, 10-12 cm long, with heart-shaped, overlapping, green and salmon or brownish-red bracts which remain on the plant for a long time; the small white flowers with purple spots on the lower lip fall off fairly quickly.

This plant requires a light, airy spot in full sunlight. In summer, protect only from very bright light. Ordinary potting compost with some peat and sharp sand. Water liberally during the growing period and feed once a week. 16-22° C; cooler in winter (12-16° C), and give less water (but the soil should not dry out). Repot in spring. For bushy growth, prune back about two-thirds of plant. Pinch out growing tips in summer and remove first flowers. Propagate from cuttings (summer) and seed (spring/summer).

*Beloperone guttata "Inge",
Shrimp plant*

Billbergia

○ ↕ 45-90 ○ ◐ ✿ 5-8 🌡 ✂

Billbergia is indigenous in tropical and subtropical regions in America. It comprises 60 epiphytic species and numerous hybrids. This is a bushy evergreen plant with cylindrical rosettes of stalkless, leathery, dark green leaves, rough on the underside and with a serrated margin, hanging or erect flowers and brightly coloured bracts from which the blue, purple and sometimes white or red flowerheads or clusters protrude.
B. nutans (Queen's tears) has large rosettes of narrow, lanceolate, olive or bronze-green leaves, 30-45 cm long, with serrated, curved tips, pinkish-red bracts and elegantly curved pinkish-red flowerheads with beautifully marked blooms. It constantly forms new rosettes. There is no fixed flowering time; it flowers early in spring if placed in a warm spot in winter, or late in summer, after a cool spot in winter.
B. pyramidalis (syn. *B. thyrsoidea*) has rosettes of lanceolate leaves, 45-60 cm long, and pinkish-red and white flowerheads;

some cultivars have red or multicoloured flowerheads. It has a very short flowering time.
B. x windii is crossed from the parent plant, *B. nutans*. It is very hardy, and forms new rosettes of leaves extremely quickly by means of numerous runners. Several of these can flower at the same time.
This is an easy plant to grow in a light spot, protected from bright sunlight. Airy soil, e.g., a mixture of leaf-mould, fern root, and sphagnum moss. 18-20° C. Water regularly with lime-free water, and add plant food (half concentration) to water in the cylinder once a month. Spray in hot weather. In winter, minimum 12° C, less water, no plant food. When it is flowering, place plant in a darker spot. Remove dead flowerheads. Repot every year, propagate by removing young rosettes when they are half the height of the parent plant.

Bougainvillea

⚘ ↕ 30-50 ○ ✲ 5-9 ! ⬈ ✂

Bougainvillea originally comes from South America, particularly Brazil, but it is also very common in southern Europe, where it flowers profusely, usually as a climbing garden plant. In colder regions it is an ideal house plant for sunny spots, either as a small shrub or trained on wire hoops. Before the plant is sold it is immersed in a growth solution in order to prevent the buds dropping off.
Outside, this climbing shrub grows to a height of 4 m. It has thorny branches, oval, pointed leaves and masses of small white flowers with brightly coloured pink, red, purple or orange bracts on young shoots.
B. glabra, 4-5 m tall, is a powerful climbing plant with pinkish-red bracts in summer.
B. spectabilis is a strong, fast-growing plant, with hairy, dark green leaves and reddish-purple bracts. The two species have been crossed to produce many cultivars with white, yellowish-orange, pink, red and purple bracts, such as *Bougainvillea* "Alexandra", with bright purple bracts; "Dania", dark pink; "Purple Dwarf", purple; "Sanderiana", bluish purple.
This plant requires a sunny, airy spot and moist soil, rich in humus. Water liberally and spray during flowering period, and give additional plant food every week. In winter it requires a light spot, cooler (5-10° C), less water (soil should not dry out), no plant food. The leaves may be allowed to drop off. Gradually start to give more water when the buds appear on the young shoots (watering before this inhibits flowering). Pinch out tips regularly for more prolific flowering. Prune back (hard) immediately after flowering. Repot every two or three years in spring. Propagate from cuttings of slightly woody stems (spring); this is fairly difficult, provide bottom heat (30° C) and use rooting powder.

Bougainvillea

Browallia
Bush violet

• ↕ 30-75 ◐ ✲ all year round ! ⬈ ✂

Browallia is indigenous in tropical regions of South America. The plant flowers in summer and can grow to a height of 1.5 m in its country of origin, though cultivars are not so tall. By sowing seed in July/August, it can also flower in winter. This is a herbaceous plant which branches out. It has flexible stems, dark green, smooth-edged leaves in whorls or placed irregularly, trumpet-shaped blue, purple or white flowers with a long, narrow, tube-shaped calyx, and five unequal, spreading petals, which grow singly in the leaf axilla, or in clusters facing the same way.
B. speciosa is a semi-shrub which grows 50-75 cm tall when cultivated, with hairless stems which are woody at the base, pointed, oval dark green leaves, and single, short-stemmed bluish-violet flowers with a white heart and smooth petals; *B. speciosa* "Alba", entirely white flowers; "Major", larger blue flowers, usually grown from seed as annuals.
B. viscosa is an annual, 30-60 cm tall. The entire plant is sticky, with numerous coarse, hairy, long oval leaves, and dark blue flowers with a white heart, and deeply indented petals.
This plant requires a cool, light spot, and porous potting compost rich in humus. Keep moderately moist and feed once a fortnight. 15-18° C. Pinch out tips regularly and remove dead flowers immediately. Propagate from seed at 20° C (flowers appear after approximately 4 months) and from (top) cuttings.

Brunfelsia

Yesterday, today and tomorrow

60 3/4-8

Brunfelsia is indigenous in tropical regions in Central and South America.
It is an evergreen plant with lanceolate, shiny green leaves, a long tubular corolla, and large (light) blue, yellow or white, dish-shaped blooms.
B. pauciflora var. *calycina* is a spreading plant with dark green leaves which are pale green on the underside, and violet flowers with a white heart. *B. pauciflora* "Eximia" (syn. *B. calycina*, *B. eximia*) has beautifully fragrant flowers which are a violet purplish to white colour.
This plant requires a light spot protected from direct sunlight and good, moist, non-alkaline potting compost. Water regularly during the growing and flowering period. Constant temperature (20° C). Feed weekly. High humidity (spray). To promote flowering, place the plant in a cooler spot while it is resting (November to January), maximum 15° C, some light, less water. Gradually increase warmth, give more water and feed with nitrogen-rich plant food for leaves with a good colour. Repot if necessary in spring, prune back well. Propagate from top cuttings or stem cuttings.

Brunfelsia pauciflora var. calycina, Yesterday, today and tomorrow

Browallia speciosa, Bush violet

Calathea

○ ⊘ ↕ 30-40 ✦ 3-9 ⍦ ⊰

Calathea is indigenous in the tropical
rainforests of South America. There are
about 350 species, of which a number are
sold as pot plants, mainly because of their
leaves, such as *C. makoyana* and *C. picturata*.
Only one species, *B. crocata*, flowers indoors.
B. crocata has lanceolate/oval shiny, dark
green leaves which have long stems and are
almost horizontal, and long, erect, flowering
stems with orangey-yellow, saffron-coloured
flowers at the ends. The time at which they
flower depends on the temperature during
the period of cultivation.
The plant requires a light, warm spot (in
winter), or a shady spot (in summer), and
good potting compost with some extra peat,
which is always kept moist. Spray regularly
with water low in lime. Give additional
plant food every week during the growing
period (half concentration). High humidity,
place plant on an upturned saucer in a dish
of water. In winter, water sparingly during
resting period. Repot in early spring, and
propagate by dividing new shoots with at
least three leaves. Plant in a shallow pot.

Calathea crocata

Calceolaria
Slipper flower

· ↕ 25-50 ⊘ ✦ 10-5 ⍦ ⊰

The name *Calceolaria* comes from the Latin
word "calceolus" (shoe, slipper), and the
English name, Slipper plant, is a reference
to the curiously shaped flowers. The plant is
indigenous in the mountain forests of South
America. As a result of special methods of
cultivation, a number of species are available
as house plants almost all the year round
(slightly less from June to September), but
after flowering, the plant dies. Hybrids of
the "Multiflora" variety are particularly
cultivated.
This is a herbaceous or woody-stemmed
plant with large, oval leaves in whorls, and

Campanula
Star of Bethlehem

○ ↕ 30 ○ ⊘ ⊛ 7-9 ▯ ⬭

*middle: Calceolaria,
Slipper flower*

Campanula (means bell) is indigenous in the temperate regions of the northern hemisphere, particularly in Mediterranean regions. There are many species which are suitable as garden plants, but *C. isophylla* is a plant which is suitable for growing indoors and flowers profusely. It is available all the year round by cultivating it in artificial light.
C. isophylla, Star of Bethlehem, has creeping, hairy stems and large pale blue flowers. The five petals are fused in a star shape; *C. isophylla* "Alba" has white flowers: "Mayi" has slightly larger, purplish-blue flowers.
This plant requires a light spot, protected from sunlight, and nutritious soil, rich in humus, e.g., a mixture of leaf-mould, clay and old manure. Water liberally, slightly more in hot weather/a warm spot, and slightly less in a cooler spot. Give additional plant food every week during the growing period. Remove dead flowers. Prune back plant after flowering. Place in a light, cool spot (8-10° C) in winter. Repot in spring. Propagate from top cuttings of new shoots (spring) at 10-15° C, with some growth medium.

*Campanula isophylla,
Star of Bethlehem*

broad, oval, brightly coloured blooms, sometimes with tiger spots or marbled, with a pouch-shaped lower lip.
The flowers of *C. crenatiflora* hybrids (syn. *Calceolaria x herbeohybrida*) and *Calceolaria* "Multiflora" have red, orange or yellow flowers which can have yellow, red, brown or purple blotches or markings to a greater or lesser extent. The plants flower for about 4 weeks.
They require a light, draught-free spot, protected from direct sunlight, which is moderately warm (16-18° C), and special, extra-acid potting compost (the leaves turn yellow if there is an iron deficiency). Water regularly and spray (not on the flowers), remove blooms when they have finished flowering, and discard the plant after flowering. Sensitive to aphids.

25

Celosia

Celosia
Plume flower

· ↕ 15-60 ○ ❀ 6-9 🏺 ✂

The only cultivar of *Celosia*, which is indigenous in Indonesia, is *C. argentea*; the varieties available are divided into two groups: "Plumosa" varieties, with plume-shaped flowerheads, and "Cristata" varieties, with a convoluted flowerhead. The period of flowering depends on when it is sown. The plant dies after it has flowered. *C. argentea* "Cristata" has a "cockscomb", a broad, convoluted flowerhead, approximately 30 cm tall, in many different colours, red, pink, orange, purple, cream and yellow; "Cristata Jewel Box" has heavy, beautifully coloured flowerheads up to 15 cm tall. It requires a great deal of fresh air. *C. argentea* "Plumosa" (Plume flower) has pale green or golden-yellow leaves, and many large, elegant, pyramid-shaped, red, yellow or golden plumes. It is also suitable as a border plant or for cut flowers. This plant requires a very light spot, but no bright sunlight, and nutritious, well-drained soil which is always kept moist, but not too wet. Feed regularly, discard after flowering. Propagate from seed (February/March or April/May).

Clerodendrum thomsonea,
Glory Bower

26

x Citrofortunella

🌱 ↕ 75-300 ○ 🪣 ◁

x Citrofortunella originates from China, and is widely cultivated in the Philippines. It is (probably) a hybrid of *Fortunella margarita* (kumquat) and *Citrus reticulata* (tangerine) and is also sold under its old name, *Citrus microcarpa*.

x *C. microcarpa* (syn. x *C. mitis*) is an evergreen shrub up to 5 m tall, with prickly, branching stems, with shiny green leathery, oval to lanceolate leaves, 5-10 cm long, and orangey-yellow, orange-like fruit up to 4 cm in diameter, and beautifully fragrant white clusters of flowers several times a year. The fruit soon appears on young plants and can remain on the branches for a long time, so that the plants often have fruit and flowers at the same time. In summer it can stand outside in a sheltered spot. The fruit is suitable only for making marmalade; for more fruit, pollinate the flowers with a brush.

This plant requires a light spot, not too warm, and protected against bright sunlight. The soil should not be too acid, e.g., a mixture of leaf-mould or peat, sharp sand, clay, and old cow manure. Water liberally in summer and spray frequently (not on the flowers). Feed every week. 15-18° C, never above 25° C, cooler in winter (8-10° C), less water, no plant food. Yellow leaves means there is too much lime. Prune back for bushier growth. Only repot if necessary; the roots are very vulnerable. Propagate from top cuttings (summer) and from pips.

x Citrofortunella

Clerodendrum
Glory Bower

🌱 ↕ 30-150 ○ ⊘ ❀ 4-9 ! 🪣 ◁

The name *Clerodendrum* is derived from the Greek words "kleros" (fate, chance) and "dendron" (tree), which refer to the use of both the toxic and healing qualities of some of the approximately 400 species which are found throughout the tropics and subtropics; several species are suitable for growing indoors.

This is a climbing plant, shrub or (woody-stemmed) tree with whorls or clusters of leaves, and clusters of flowers at the ends of the stems. It has brightly coloured, bell-shaped flowers with a large tube-shaped corolla, protruding stamens and berry-like fruit.

C. x speciosum, a hybrid of *C. splendens*, which has bright red flowers, and *C. thomsonea*, which has erect, dark green, heart-shaped leaves and flowers profusely with pinkish-red, erect flowers.

C. thomsonea is a climbing plant with bare stems and whorls of dark green, oval, pointed leaves, and flowers at the end of the stems and the leaf axilla, with a white pentagonal calyx and fiery red flowers with strikingly long stamens.

This plant requires a very light spot, protected from bright sunlight, and potting compost rich in humus, e.g, equal parts of leaf-mould, clay and old manure. Keep moist evenly, spray frequently for high humidity and feed every week during growing period. 16-30° C, cooler in winter (10-12° C), and less water. Repot after flowering. Press soil down firmly and prune back the plant (February/March). Propagate from cuttings and seed.

27

Columnea gloriosa

Clivia

⭕ ↕ 30-60 🔵 ❁ 4-8 ❗ 🪣 ✂

Clivia is indigenous in South Africa, particularly in Natal. There are only three species, of which *C. miniata* was the first to be cultivated in England in 1862. This plant has thick, fleshy roots, from which the shiny, dark green, strap-like leaves develop in pairs. It has sturdy stems with clusters of trumpet-shaped flowers at the ends.
C. miniata, Kaffir Lily, has thick leaves, 30-60 cm long, which grow in two directions and orangey-red clusters of flowers.
C. nobilis has long, blunt leaves with rough margins, and hanging, reddish-yellow umbels with more, but smaller flowers.
This plant requires a light, shady place, out of direct sunlight. Do not move it. It requires good, porous, potting compost rich in humus, e.g., equal parts of leaf-mould, clay and rotted manure. The plant needs a lot of fresh air. Water liberally during the growing and flowering period. Do not leave water in the pot (root rot). Spray with tepid water. Feed every two weeks from February to August. 18-22° C. To flower profusely, it requires a good period of rest of at least 2 months from October, cooler (6-10° C), with little water and no plant food. Place in a warmer spot and give more water only when the flowering stalk is 15-18 cm long. Yellow leaves means that there is too much sunlight and the water is too cold. Repot every three years immediately after the plant has flowered. Take great care (to prevent damage to roots) and plant in a small, rather than large pot. Propagate from seed (this takes a long time), and by removing runners.

Columnea

⭕ ↕ 50-200 🔵 ❁ various 🪣 ✂

Columnea is indigenous in the tropical rainforests of Central America. It comprises about 160 epiphytic varieties, which are often cultivated as hanging plants. With proper care, these pot plants can flower for several months. It is an evergreen semi-shrub, with trailing stems, and short-stemmed whorls of leaves which can be smooth or hairy. It has a long flowering period, numerous large, orange-coloured, sometimes yellow, tube-shaped flowers, standing alone or in groups in the leaf axilla.

C. x banksii has sturdy stems up to 1 m long, small, fleshy, smooth dark green leaves which are reddish on the underside, and orangey-red flowers with yellow stripes in spring.
C. gloriosa, Goldfish plant, has limp stems, small, hairy, purplish leaves, and large, scarlet flowers with pale yellow blotches in autumn.
C. hirta has creeping stems, 70 cm long, stiff, long, oval, very hairy leaves, and large red flowers at the end of the winter.
C. microphylla has thin stems up to 2 m long, small, round, reddish, hairy leaves, and orangey-red flowers with a yellow throat in spring and summer; "Variegata" has coloured leaves and orange flowers.
This plant requires a light spot protected from bright sunlight, and airy, slightly acid potting compost, e.g, a mixture of leaf-mould and peat. During the growing period, keep moist at all times, but not too wet (root rot). Water regularly and spray with soft water (not on hairy leaves and flowers, this produces blotches). Feed once a week. For high humidity, the plant can be placed on an upturned saucer in a dish of water. 18-24° C. Prune back after flowering. For flowers to form, allow a resting period of 1-2 months in winter, cooler (16-18° C), less water (but the soil should not dry out). No plant food. Repot if necessary in a shallow pot. Propagate from cuttings after flowering (spring/summer) with several cuttings in a pot of sandy soil.

Clivia miniata

Cuphea ignea, Cigar plant

Cuphea
Cigar plant

· 🌿 ↕ 15-40 ○ ✿ 6-10 🪣

Cuphea is mainly indigenous in America, particularly in Mexico. It comprises about 200 species. A number are cultivated in western Europe for growing in gardens, often as annuals, but *C. ignea* is also a very attractive pot plant.
C. ignea, Cigar plant, has erect, branching, brownish stems, whorls of (un)stalked, oval, pointed leaves, and long, red, tubular flowers with a white mouth and a black top.
This plant requires a cool, very light spot, protected from bright sunlight, and normal, nutritious potting compost. Keep moist at all times. Water regularly during the growing period and feed every two weeks. The plant is usually discarded after flowering, but it is possible to grow new plants from cuttings. Also propagate from seed (January/February).

*Cyclamen "Rosa
von Zehlendorf"*

Cyclamen

 25-40 9-3

Cyclamen is mainly indigenous in
Mediterranean regions. It comprises 17 very
similar species. The popular house plant is
descended mainly from *C. persicum*, which
was first cultivated in England in 1731.
The process of selection, cross-fertilization
and hybridization has produced an
extremely large and varied range.
C. persicum is 25 cm tall, with a round,
tuberous, hairless rootstock, long stems, and
oval or heart-shaped leaves growing in
rosettes. They are dark green with silvery
markings, reddish on the underside and
with serrated margins. The long, hollow,
erect flowering stems have striking single
pink, blue or white blooms at the top,
usually consisting of five petals, one of
which is pendent; there are many varieties
with flowers in all sorts of different shades
from white to bright red, often with a
contrastingly coloured centre. They can be
subdivided into varieties with fringed or
smooth large flowers ("Vuurbaak",
salmon-coloured flowers, "Rosa von
Zehlendorf", pale pink); varieties with small
flowers, 15 cm tall ("Wellensiek"), which
often has slightly fragrant smaller flowers;
"Rococco" with fringed petals in a more
horizontal position; "Victoria", fringed
petals with the centre and leaf margin in the
same colour; double flowers: nowadays
there are also "mini" cyclamens available,
such as "Anneli", with white flowers.
This plant requires a cool, slightly shady
spot, and fertile, well-drained soil, e.g.,
equal parts of leaf-mould, sharp sand, clay
and old cow manure. Water liberally with
soft, tepid water during flowering period.
Remove surplus water from the saucer. Do
not water in the leaf rosettes (to prevent
rotting). Immerse once a week, feed every
two weeks, remove blooms when they have

finished flowering, and yellow leaves with the stem at the base (to prevent rotting). 15-18° C. After flowering (spring), keep tuber in the pot in a cool spot (10° C), water occasionally, and do not feed. Repot in autumn, place in a slightly warmer spot and give more water. Propagate from seed (January/February or August/September) in acid soil.

Cymbidium

○ ↕ 40-60(-150) ◉ ✿ 11-1 🪣 ✂

Cymbidium is indigenous in Asia and Australia. It comprises about 40 epiphytic and terrestrial species. A number of hybrids are common in this part of the world as cut flowers, but some, including the miniature *Cymbidiums,* can also flower for several weeks as a house plant. The plant is then discarded or kept in a cold or heated greenhouse.
This is an orchid with a creeping rootstock and pseudobulbs encased in leaf sheaths, long, narrow, curved leaves, and long or short, erect or pendent flowering stems with several rather waxy flowers on every stem. It is available in many colours and colour combinations, with two rings of three petals, with the middle leaf of the inner ring shaped into a strikingly shaped and/or coloured lip. *Cymbidium* hybrids with large flowers require a great deal of space because of the size of the leaf; miniature *Cymbidiums* are much more practical, with white, yellow, green or pink flowers and beautiful markings on the lip, e.g., "Annan Cooksbridge", which has dark pink flowers with black markings on the lip; "King Arthur", with greenish-red petals and a creamy-red spotted lip; "Palleas", reddish-brown.
This winter-flowering plant requires an airy, light or slightly shady spot, and moist, well-drained soil, e.g., a mixture of light clay and sphagnum moss. Feed once a week during the growing period. Minimum 20° C, at night 16° C, all the year round. During the resting period (from February), slightly cooler, less water. Repot every 2 years after flowering. Propagate by dividing pseudobulbs.

Cyclamen

Cymbidium

Dendranthema morifolium hybrid

Dendranthema

⚘ ↕ 15-75 ◉ ⊛ all year round ▣ ⊠

Dendranthema is much better known under its synonym, *Chrysanthemum*. It is indigenous from western to south-eastern Europe, and from central to eastern Asia. The pot plant, chrysanthemum, *D. indicum*, originates from China and Japan. The plant is available in full flower all year round, because of artificially reducing the hours of daylight and treating with growth-inhibiting chemicals. It is discarded when it has flowered and it is difficult to keep. *D. indicum*, syn. *Chrysthanemum indicum* is a branching, bushy, shrub-like plant with a sharp, pungent fragrance. It has coarsely serrated or lobed, greyish-green, slightly hairy leaves whose size depends on the size of the flowers, and white, yellow, orange, pink, red or purple blooms in plumes or clusters. They can be large, medium or small, in bunches, with single, double or compound flowers; with ray flowers, or spherical flowers, such as "Applause", with double yellow flowers; "Draga", large yellow flowers, "Pink Arola", double purple flowers, "Surf", white flowers, "Tan", bronze flowers.
This plant requires a light, cool spot, out of direct sunlight. Water moderately, do not let soil dry out. Feed once a week and remove blooms when they have finished flowering.

Duchesnea indica,
Ornamental strawberry

Duchesnea
Ornamental strawberry

○ ↕ 20-25 ◉ ⊛ 6-9 ▣ ⊠

The fact that *Duchesnea*, which is indigenous in Southern Asia, is related to *Fragaria*, the Alpine strawberry, is clear from the false fruit, though that of Duchesnea is tasteless and dry, and only has ornamental value.
D. indica is the best known of the six species and is also grown indoors.
D. indica, the Indian strawberry, has a short rootstock, long- stemmed, oval, serrated leaves which grow in threes, and runners with long-stemmed, single, yellow flowers 1.5 cm across, with green bracts and many stamens and pistils. The small, red false fruit, up to 1 cm in diameter, appear later (the pips are the true fruit).
This is a hanging plant which can be trained around iron hoops. It requires a light spot and moist, nutritious spoil. Water regularly and spray. Keep cool in winter, repot if necessary. Propagate by removing runners which have taken root, and from seed (April).

Euphorbia

◦ ⛏ ↕ 30-80 ○ ◉ ✿ 5-9/10-1 ! 🪣 ⊠

Euphorbias are found all over the world and comprise both annuals and perennials, succulents, cacti, shrubs and trees. They all have a poisonous milky juice, and therefore house plants should be placed out of the reach of children. It may be a good idea to wear gloves when repotting etc.

The small, insignificant flowers are surrounded by brightly coloured bracts, like petals, which determine the plant's ornamental value.

E. milii, the Crown of Thorns, is a succulent which can grow to a height of 1 m, with woody, round, branching, dark brown, spiny stems, and oval or spatulate blunt leaves with sticky flowering stems, and bright red bracts. There are also pale red, yellow and cream-coloured varieties. It requires a sunny, warm spot, cactus soil or potting compost with extra sand. During the growing period, keep fairly moist and feed once a week. 20° C. Water sparingly in winter (too much water causes the leaves to fall), and place in a cooler spot. Repot every 2 or 3 years (April). Propagate from cuttings (spring). It is best not to move the plant (to prevent leaves forming).

E. pulcherrima, "Poinsettia", flowers in winter and is an evergreen shrub, growing up to 3 m in the wild. It has erect, woody (un)branched stems without spines, long-stemmed, oval or lanceolate pointed leaves, and blood-red, pink, white, yellow or bicoloured bracts which retain their colour for a long time; "Angelika", dark-red; "Dorothy", salmon-coloured; "Marble", yellow, with pale red blotches; "Regina", yellow with green veins; "Sub-ji-bi", large, bright red flowers.

This plant requires a very light spot protected from direct sunlight, and soil rich in humus, e.g., a mixture of leaf-mould, clay and old cow manure. Spray regularly with tepid water during the flowering period (watch out for root rot). In heated rooms, spray occasionally. Feed every week. The plant is often discarded when the bracts have lost their colour and have fallen off. If not, it is possible to reduce the hours of daylight so that it will flower again at Christmas. Prune back and brush the cuts with powdered charcoal. Repot, shake off old earth, and place in a cooler spot (17° C) for about 2 months. Allow a maximum of 8-10 hours of daylight per day. Pinch out tips occasionally. Keep relatively dry. When the leaves change colour, you have been successful, and gradually water and feed as usual.

Euphorbia

Euphorbia pulcherrima

Eustoma

Eustoma

•• | 30-70 ○ ◉ ❀ 5-9 ▯ ◁

Eustoma is indigenous in warm regions of
North and South America and the West
Indies. The name is derived from the Greek
words "eu" (good, beautiful) and "stoma"
(mouth), which refer to the beautiful
wide-open flowers which are also very
popular as cut flowers when they are
known as *Lisianthus*. Low-growing varieties
of *E. grandiflorum* are particularly popular as
house plants; under favourable conditions
the plant lasts for 6-8 weeks.
E. grandiflorum (syn. *Lisianthus russelianus*),
70-100 cm tall, has erect, branching stems,
oval, pointed leaves in pairs, with smooth
margins, and long, flowering stems with
deep purple, pale pink or white flowers
which grow singly or in clusters, with
4-6 wide, bell-shaped, spreading petals. The
young buds are enclosed by narrow, pointed
sepals. There are varieties with single and
double flowers, as well as bicoloured purple
and white flowers.
Place in a light spot protected against bright

Exacum

sunlight, and not too warm (18-20° C).
Water regularly with soft water and spray
occasionally (not the flowers). Remove wilted
flowers and discard plant after flowering.

Exacum

●● ⬆ 20-35 ⊘ ✿ 7-10 🪣 ✂

Exacum is indigenous in tropical and
subtropical regions of Asia and Africa,
amongst other places. *E. affine* is the main
species sold as a house plant. Although it is
a biennial plant, it is not usually worth the
trouble of keeping, and is usually discarded
after flowering.
E. affine has erect, bare stems which branch
out, with pairs of small, oval, pointed,
slightly fleshy, fresh green leaves, and
fragrant, star-shaped, lilac-blue flowers,
1 cm wide, with bright yellow stamens;
there are also white or lilac-pink varieties
with either single or double flowers.
This plant requires a light, draught-free
spot, protected from bright sunlight and
regular fresh air. The soil should be
nutritious (the plants can be repotted after
purchase into potting compost with extra
peat and sand). Keep moist, but not too wet
(root rot), feed every two weeks and remove
blooms when they have flowered. Propagate
from seed (February/March).

*Gardenia jasminoides
"Fortuniana"*

Gardenia

 ⬆ 60-150 ○ ✿ 6-8 🪣 ✂

Gardenia is indigenous in tropical and
subtropical regions of Asia and Africa. In
the past the heavy, fragrant flowers of
G. jasminoides were worn as buttonholes,
but nowadays the fragrance is sometimes
considered overpowering.
G. jasminoides is the only species cultivated
as a house plant. It is an evergreen shrub,
100-150 cm tall, with short-stemmed,
leathery, shiny dark green, oval to lanceolate
leaves with smooth margins, 10 cm long,
which grow in pairs or whorls. The

flowering stems grow from the leaf axilla
with double white or cream blooms, 6-8 cm
across, which grow on their own and have
thick, solid, waxy petals.
This plant requires a very light spot
protected against bright sunlight, and soil
which is poor in lime and rich in humus,
e.g., a mixture of leaf-mould, clay, sharp
sand, and old cow manure. When the plant
is flowering, keep fairly moist, but not too
wet. Water frequently with soft, tepid water,
and immerse regularly. Feed every two
weeks. For high humidity, spray the plant
(but not the flowers). Constant temperature,
20-22° C and 16° C at night. In winter it
has a resting period. Place in a cooler spot,
(12-15° C - if it is too warm, the buds will
not develop). Keep slightly moist. Prune
back older plants (April). Repot (taking care
of the roots) and gradually place in a
warmer spot. Yellow leaves mean the soil is
too wet and the water is too cold. Repot
every 2-3 years. Propagate from
non-flowering top cuttings
(February-March) and from seed (this is
difficult).

Gerbera

○ | ↑ | 30-50 ○ ✿ 6-9 ⚗ ⊰

Although *Gerbera*, which is indigenous in Asia, Africa and Madagascar, is well known as a plant for cut flowers, there are a number of species which make good house plants. The most important ancestor of the present varieties is *G. jamesonii*. They are sometimes available under a group name, by name or by colour.

G. jamesonii hybrids are very hairy plants with root rosettes. Numerous long-stemmed, oval or lanceolate, pinnate, lobed leaves, up to 30 cm long, and daisy-like flowerheads 12-16 cm across, at the end of long leafless stems, in all sorts of shades of red, orange, yellow, pink, cream, white, sometimes with a contrasting heart. There are also double varieties.

This plant requires a light, sunny, warm spot, and dry, slightly manured soil, rich in sulphur. Water liberally in summer, feed every two weeks and spray (not on the flowers). 20-24 ° C. Remove some leaves in autumn, and keep for the winter in a cool, frost-free spot (5° C). Keep moderately moist. Repot in April/May. Gradually place in a warmer spot and give more water. Propagate from seed and by dividing the plant (spring).

Gerbera

Gloriosa
Glory lily

🖐 ↕ 100-500 ◯ ⊘ ✿ 5-7 ! 🪴 ✄

Gloriosa is indigenous in tropical regions of East Africa and Asia. Nowadays it is considered to comprise only one species, viz., *G. superba*, which is often trained along a trellis or iron hoops. The whole plant is poisonous.
G. superba (syn. *G. rothschildiana*) is a climbing plant which branches out, with herbaceous stems, 1-5 m long, with shiny, green, narrow, smooth-edged leaves in pairs or spread out with tendrils at the top, and 12-15 cm long flower stems, each with a single lily-like flower with orangey-red wavy petals, folded back with a yellow edge.
This plant requires a very light warm spot and nutritious, well-drained soil, e.g., a mixture of leaf-mould, loam, sharp sand and some old cow manure. Keep moist by watering regularly with tepid water and feed once a week (half concentration). For high humidity, spray frequently (not the flowers). Remove blooms as soon as they have finished flowering. In the autumn the plant dies down. Allow tuber to dry out in the pot and store at 10-12° C. In spring, remove old earth and carefully repot the tuber in shallow potting compost (taking care not to damage the growing tip). Propagate from seed (this takes a long time), or by (carefully) dividing the tuber.

Gloxinia

○ ↕ 40-50 ⊘ ✿ 5-10 ▽

Gloxinia is indigenous in tropical America. For some time it has comprised only six species, and the house plant generally sold as gloxinia is not one of these; it is now classified under *Sinningia*. *G. sylvatica* is an attractive house plant which is becoming increasingly popular and flowers for several months.

G. sylvatica (syn. *Seemannia latifolia*, *Seemannia sylvatica*) has scaly rootstocks, brownish-red, sometimes hairy stems, short-stemmed leaves with short stalks, and long-stemmed, lantern-like, orangey-red tubular flowers with a yellow throat, 2 cm long, growing singly.

This plant requires a light, warm, draught-free spot out of direct sunlight, and slightly acid, lime-free soil, rich in humus, e.g., equal parts of leaf-mould, peat, sharp sand and some cow manure. Water liberally with tepid water (cold water on the leaves produces spots); add some plant food to the water every two weeks. 20-30° C. For high humidity, plants can be placed on an upturned saucer in a dish of water. After flowering (September), the plant dies off above the ground. Cut away stems. Allow to dry out and store in winter at 15° C. In January/February remove old earth and repot in fresh compost at 1-2 cm. Keep moist at all times. 18-20° C. Add some manure after 6-8 weeks. Propagate by dividing tubers, from cuttings and from seed.

Gloxinia sylvatica

Gomphrena

· ↕ 30-60 ○ ✿ 4-8 ⬚ ⊰

Gomphrena is mainly indigenous in tropical and subtropical America. It comprises about 100 species, of which *G. globosa* is the only species to be cultivated. The flowers are sold as cut flowers and dried flowers. It can flower from 4-12 weeks indoors.

G. globosa has herbaceous, strongly branching stems, 30-60 cm long, covered with soft hair, and pairs of lanceolate or oval leaves, 5-10 cm long, with hairy margins, which are undivided and half enclose the stem; spherical, purple or purplish-red blooms at the top of the stem and flowers surrounded by bicoloured bracts. There are also varieties in white, pink, salmon, orange, red and purple, such as the purple-coloured "Buddy".

This plant requires a light, sunny spot and nutritious, fairly moist soil. Water regularly and feed once a week. 18-24° C. After flowering the plant dies down and can be discarded. Propagate from seed (March/April).

Gomphrena globosa

*Gomphrena globosa
"Buddy and Cissy"*

39

Guzmania

○ ↕ 40-75 ◉ ✿ all year round ⌷ ✂

Guzmania is indigenous in tropical rainforests in northern South America and in Costa Rica. It comprises about 125 species, and a large number of hybrids which are either epiphytic, living on other plants, or terrestrial (living on the ground). The fairly thin, smooth-edged leaves grow in rosettes and form a cylinder which serves as a reservoir for nutrients.

The characteristic bloom appears in the middle of the rosette or on a stem with strikingly coloured bracts which last for a long time, and usually with less striking, yellow or white flowers fused in a tube, which often quickly disappear. After flowering once, the rosette of leaves slowly dies down, but a new plant can fairly easily be grown from the young rosettes of the parent plant. Growth regulators make it possible to obtain flowering plants all year round.

G. dissitiflora has a bloom with a long stem and narrow, reddish bracts and small white flowers.

G. lingulata (Scarlet Star) is an important ancestor of many hybrids with rosettes 80-90 cm wide and 30 cm tall, and narrow, ribbed, shiny bright green leaves with a red, stripy base, and a flowering stem 30 cm long, with fiery red triangular bracts, and a yellowish-white cluster of flowers in the heart; *G. lingulata* var. *minor* (syn. *G. minor*) has small, compact rosettes up to 20 cm tall, and an inflorescence of white flowers of about the same height, with bracts varying from yellow and orange to bright red.

G. monostachya (syn. *G. tricolor*) has broad

Guzmania lingulata

Guzmania minor

Guzmania

rosettes 40 cm tall, with narrow, slightly
curved leaves, and a taller, flowering stem,
with white flowers hidden amongst broad,
oval, pointed bracts which are
greenish-brown or black at the base, and
bright red to orange further up.
G. musaica has pale green rosettes with
beautiful reddish-brown and dark green
markings, and stiff, broad leaves, 50-60 cm
long. The flowering stem has a compact
inflorescence of yellowish-white flowers and
short, red bracts. The attractive markings on
the leaves are extremely decorative.
G. sanguinea has strikingly coloured rosettes.
Before flowering, the inner leaves are
yellow, yellowish-green and ruby red.
The inflorescence has no stem.
G. wittmickii has long flowering stems and an
open inflorescence of narrow, red or reddish-
purple bracts, and white, slightly lilac flowers.
Some of the hybrids include: *Guzmania*
"Amaranth", with a long-stemmed,
purplish-red bloom; "Atilla", with a
long-stemmed, open, orangey-red bloom;
"Empire", with rosette-shaped, bright red
blooms; "Grand Prix", long-stemmed, bright
red bloom; "Remembrance", with
rosette-shaped red and yellow blooms.
This plant requires a slightly shady spot in
summer and a fairly light spot in winter.
For high humidity, place the plant on an
upturned saucer in a dish of water. Use
special orchid soil or an acid, airy mixture
of sphagnum moss, fern root, sharp sand,
peat and rotted beech leaves. Keep
moderately moist and water liberally with
soft, tepid water during the growing period,
also in the rosette (this should be emptied
every few weeks and filled with fresh water).
Feed once a fortnight (half concentration).
Do not water in the centre while the plant
is flowering. In winter, minimum temperature
18° C, and stop spraying. Repot in spring
when the pot has become too small.
Propagate by dividing side shoots which
have taken root; do not remove young
rosettes until the parent plant dies off.

Helleborus

○ ⬆ 15-30 ⊘ ✤ 11-12 ! ⬛ ✂

Helleborus is mainly indigenous in Central
and Southern Europe and Asia Minor.
H. niger subsp. *niger* is the main species sold
as a flowering plant or as cut flowers during
the Christmas season. It is usually sold
without leaves; the old leaves are cut away
to promote flowering and the new leaves
still have to form. The length of time it can
be kept depends on the temperature (not

too warm).
H. niger subsp. *niger* is an evergreen plant
which grows up to a height of 30 cm, with
compound, leathery leaves developing from
the root, and broad, cuneate leaflets,
serrated at the top. The virtually leafless
flowering stems are erect and protrude
above the leaves. They have 1-3 bright
white, dish-shaped flowers, 8-9 cm in
diameter, which turn pink and green, and
face sideways.
This plant requires a light, shady, cool spot,
5-10° C. (over 10° C reduces the flowering
period). Keep soil moist at all times and
water regularly. As the species is rather
difficult to cultivate, it is usually put out in
the garden or discarded when it has flowered.

Helleborus niger

*Hibiscus,
Rose of China*

Hibiscus
Rose of China

⛆ ↕ 30-100 ○ ✿ 4-9 ⛆ ✂

Hibiscus is indigenous in all the tropical and subtropical regions of the world. It is a very multi-faceted genus comprising about 300 species of annual and perennial shrubs and trees. As a house plant, it benefits from a rest period in winter.

H. rosa-sinesis is a tall shrub which grows to a height of a few metres in its natural habitat. It has whorls of long-stemmed, narrow or broad, oval, dark green leaves, usually with a deeply indented margin, and single, pinkish-red, funnel-shaped flowers in the leaf axilla, which grow on their own. There are several varieties with single or double flowers in lilac, yellow, white, salmon, dark red and mixed colours with frilly or smooth edges, and coloured leaves, e.g., "Bangkok", apricot with a red heart; "Helene", dark red; "Koenig", bright yellow; "Rio", pale pink; "Rosalie", salmon. This plant requires a very light, draught-free spot protected from bright sunlight, and well-drained soil, rich in humus, e.g., equal parts of clay, loam, leaf-mould and old cow manure. During the growing season keep warm (18-24° C), and moist at all times. Water regularly, spray leaves and immerse from time to time. In summer, feed once a week. When buds have formed, do not turn plant (as this causes buds to fall), and immediately remove blooms when they have finished flowering. In autumn, prune back to a third of the length, and place in a light, cooler spot (10-15° C). Warmer conditions encourages aphids. Keep moderately moist. Do not spray or feed. Repot every year in spring. Propagate from top cuttings (April to August) using rooting powder.

*Hibiscus "Paramaribo",
Rose of China*

Hippeastrum
Amaryllis

⬦ ↕ 50-70 ○ ✼ 11-4 ▯ ✂

Hippeastrum is indigenous in the arid woodlands, savanahs and rainforests in tropical and subtropical regions of South and Central America and the Caribbean. It is sometimes confused with the bulb *Amaryllis belladonna*, true amaryllis, but the latter is not suitable for growing indoors. The process of selection of *Hippeastrum* hybrids, mainly in England and the Netherlands, has produced numerous varieties with different colours and large, well-formed flowers.

Depending on the size, one or more hollow stalks develop from the bulb, with 2-4/5 large, red, pink, salmon, white or bicoloured flowers with two rings of three petals which form a tube at the base, and protruding stamens with yellow anthers. The narrow, strap-like, dark green leaves appear during or after the plant has flowered. *Hippeastrum* "Apple Blossom" is pink with white flowers; "Minerva", red with white markings; "Picotee", white with a red margin; "Red Lion", scarlet.

The bulb has a well-developed system of roots. Place in the earth almost up to the growing tip in a warm spot. Keep moderately moist at all times. When the stalk is 15-20 cm long, place in a lighter, cooler spot and give more water. When it is flowering, it should be in a cool place. Spray the leaves occasionally. After flowering, cut the stalk, discard the plant or continue to cultivate. In August (for early flowering) or September, stop watering and store the bulb in the pot for 4-5 weeks at 16° C, and 4 weeks at 23° C. Change the soil, repot if necessary, and place in a warm spot (20° C). Repot every two years, propagate from bulbils and seeds.

Hippeastrum "Pasedena", Amaryllis

Hippeastrum "Picotee", Amaryllis

43

Hoya carnosa "Exotica",
Wax plant

Hoya
Wax plant

⊙ ↕ 30-50 ○ ⊘ ⊛ 7-9 ! ⊻ ⊰

Hoya is indigenous in Southern China, the
Indonesian Archipelago, and Australia.
It owes its English name to its waxy
flowers. *Chamelaucium*, which are sold as
cut flowers, are also sold under this name.
Of the 200 species, only a few are cultivated
as pot plants. They are often trained on a
trellis or on iron hoops.
This is an evergreen climber or small shrub

Hoya bella, Wax plant

with thin stems, pairs of leathery, thick,
fleshy, undivided leaves, fragrant, pendent
clusters or umbels without stalks, of waxy
flowers with five sepals, a star-shaped,
five-lobed crown, and stamens forming
a short tube.
H. bella, the miniature wax plant, has
horizontal, later pendent stems, with thick,
oval, pointed dark green leaves with a
brown central vein, and very pendent, flat
umbels of fragrant white flowers, 1.5 cm in
diameter, with pinky-red or deep purple
hearts. Leave the stems and they will
produce new flowers in the following
season. During the growing period it should
be fairly warm, 20-22/30° C, and
moderately moist. In winter, the resting
period, 18° C, keep fairly dry for good
flower formation. Sensitive to root rot.
H. carnosa has short-stemmed, thick,
leathery, oval to lanceolate, pointed, dark
green leaves with silvery spots, and
short-stemmed, pendent umbels of larger,
flesh-coloured, fragrant flowers with a red
heart. There are cultivars with variegated
leaves, of which several flower less profusely
or not at all. Keep moist and warm in the
growing period, 16-20° C. In winter,
10-14° C, water sparingly.
This plant requires a very light spot
protected from sunlight, and airy,
well-drained soil, rich in humus, for
example, a mixture of leaf-mould, loam or
clay, sharp sand and old cow manure.
Do not allow the soil to dry out in summer,
and only feed during the flowering period,
once every three weeks. When buds have
formed, do not move the plant (this
encourages the buds to fall off). Remove
clusters with the stalks when they have
finished flowering. Repot if necessary in
spring in a fairly small pot. Propagate from
top cuttings (summer).

Hyacinthus
Hyacinth

◇ ↕ 15-25 ○ ⊘ ⊛ 11-4 ! ⊽ ⊰

Hyacinthus originates from Syria and Iraq.
It is a popular bulb in the garden, but can also
be attractive indoors; for this purpose the
bulb has had special treatment in the nursery.
H. orientalis, the only species in this genus,
is a round bulb with a pointed tip and a
rosette of leaves consisting of 4-7 fleshy,
gutter-shaped leaves with a hollow stalk
developing from the centre, with a fragrant

cluster of bell-shaped flowers in many shades of white, pink and blue. There are small, large and double varieties, e.g., "Amsterdam", pinkish-red; "Anne Marie", pink; "Blue Jacket", blue; "Carnegie", white; "Jan Bos", pinkish-red, "Ostara", purplish-blue.

Place the bulbs in earth or gravel. They should be placed in a cool dark spot to form roots. When the bud has appeared, move to a light spot, first at 18-20° C, and when the bud starts to develop, in a very light, warmer spot, 20-23° C. Keep moist at all times and water liberally. After flowering the plant is put in the garden or discarded.

Hyacinthus orientalis "Annemarie", Hyacinth

Hydrangea

Hortensia

 50-100 3-6

Hydrangea comprises 80 species.
H. macrophylla, which originates from China and Japan, is cultivated as a house plant, while various other species are well-known garden plants.
H. macrophylla is a semi-shrub with pairs of oval leaves, with serrated or lobed margins, and broad, flat or round clusters of red, blue, pink or white flowers, with four or five petals and sepals. The outer ones are often larger. There are countless cultivars, such as "Adria", which is dark pink; "Bodensee", lilac; "Leuchtfeuer", orangey-red; "Madame Emile Mouillere", white; "Masja", pink; "Renate Steiniger", pale pink; "Soeur Therese", white; "Teller" varieties, blue, red, pink and white.

This plant requires a cool, light spot, protected from direct sunlight, and acid potting compost, e.g., leaf-mould, peat, and old cow manure. Water liberally with tepid, lime-free water, or immerse occasionally. Feed with plant food, poor in lime, once a week. After flowering, which can last 6-8 weeks in a cool spot, the plant is usually discarded. With proper care it is possible to keep it: prune back and repot immediately after flowering. Some rusty nails can be added for extra iron (for blue flowers, add alum). Place in a sheltered cool spot, out of the sunlight, with a lot of fresh air, less water and no plant food. When it obviously starts to grow, give more water and feed once a week. In August/September, no plant food, less water, the leaves drop off. Store for the winter in a cool, frost-free spot (4-6° C). In February/March, place the plant in a warm spot, give more water and plant food (for early flowering in January). Older plants do not have to be repotted every year. Propagate by taking cuttings from prunings (summer).

bottom left:
Hydrangea macrophylla "Teller", Hortensia

bottom right:
Hydrangea macrophylla "Bodensee", Hortensia

Impatiens,
Busy Lizzie

Impatiens
Busy Lizzie

 15-90 5-8

Impatiens is mainly indigenous in tropical and subtropical regions of Asia and Africa; some species are found in temperate regions of the northern hemisphere. They are attractive garden and house plants. It is an annual or perennial, herbaceous plant with

succulent, usually transparent stems and serrated leaves in whorls or scattered.
The two-sided, symmetrical single or double flowers grow on their own, in groups or in clusters, on stems from the leaf axilla.
The ripe fruit spring open when touched, scattering the seeds.
I. balsamina grows wild in France and other areas in central Europe. It is a biennial, 30-80 cm tall, with reddish stems and spreading, oval or lanceolate leaves and short-stemmed, double, light red, pink, lilac and white flowers. The compact, low-growing varieties are the main ones sold as house plants.
I. walleriana (syn. *I. holstii* incl. *I. sultanii*), Busy Lizzie, is a perennial with long-stemmed, light green, oval to lanceolate serrated leaves which grow in pairs at the bottom and in whorls further up. The flowers have long or short stems and are 2-5 cm across. There are many varieties and hybrids from 50-100 cm tall, in many shades of pink, lilac, orange, red and white, or bicoloured, with single and double blooms.
Impatiens "New Guinea" hybrids are perennials with a bushy growth up to 90 cm tall, with thick swollen stems and oval to lanceolate, serrated leaves in whorls. The large, rather flat flowers usually grow on their own in bright pink to deep red shades.

Impatiens walleriana
Superelfin pink,
Busy Lizzie

The leaves are also many different colours: green, bronze, red and variegated.
This plant requires a very light spot, protected against sunlight while the buds form, with a lot of fresh air, and nutritious (standard) potting compost. Keep moist in summer and spray (not on the flowers). Feed once a week. During the resting period (winter), place in a cool spot and keep moderately moist. Regularly pinch out the tips and remove blooms when they have finished flowering. If the buds fall, this means that there is not enough light. (On dark days, switch on a light.) Repot every year in spring. Propagate from top cuttings (at any time), and from seed. The plant can be placed outside in the summer.

Ixora

 ↕ 90-120 ⊘ ⊛ 7-9 ⌂ ⌇

Ixora is indigenous in tropical areas throughout the world. In the countries of origin many species are used for medicinal purposes, particularly for toothache. Cross-fertilization has produced varieties which are attractive house plants, in contrast with the original species which require a heated greenhouse in temperate zones.
This plant has leathery, shiny green leaves, and beautiful, large, round clusters of red or orangey-red flowers consisting of four to five spreading petals which form a long tube at the base.
I. coccinea, a bushy, branching plant with oval pointed leaves and compact clusters of bright red flowers, and *I. chinensis*, with smaller clusters of flowers which turn from a yellow or orangey-yellow colour to an orangey-red, are important plants from which hybrids have been crossed.
Ixora hybrids are branching plants with beautiful shiny leaves and flowers in many shades of red, pink, orange, yellow and white. This plant requires a warm, light spot protected from bright noon sunlight, and nutritious, well-drained soil, poor in lime, e.g., a mixture of peat, leaf-mould and old cow manure. Keep moderately moist, and for high humidity, place plant on an upturned saucer in a dish of water. Spray (and water) with tepid, soft water and add plant food every two weeks. After flowering, prune back plant. During the resting period, water less and do not feed. Yellow leaves indicate an iron deficiency; use plant food containing iron. Repot if necessary in spring. Propagate from top cuttings in spring, using growth powder at 25-30° C.

Ixora coccinea

Ixora chinensis

Jasminum grandiflorum,
Jasmine

pointed terminal leaf and fragrant, clusters of white flowers, 2.5 cm across, with petals as long as the tube: "Aureovariegatum" has white flowers and yellow variegated leaves; *J. grandiflorum* (syn. *J. officinale* fa. *grandiflorum*) has larger white flowers. *J. offinicale* fa. *affine* has whitish-pink flowers. This plant requires a light spot, protected from bright sunlight, and nutritious soil, e.g., a mixture of leaf-mould, clay and old cow manure. The pot should not be too small, and a trellis is needed to train the climbing stems. During the growing period (summer), keep moist, spray with water poor in lime, and feed once a week. 18-20° C. In autumn and winter place in a cooler spot (5-10° C), water less and do not feed; February/March, gradually move to a warmer spot and give more water. If buds fall, this means that there is too little light. Repot in early spring. Do not prune back too much (buds are lost), propagate from cuttings (spring/summer), and regularly pinch out the tips of young plants.

Jasminum
Jasmine

50-400   12/3-5

Jasminum is found in tropical regions in Asia, Africa and Australia. With its wonderfully fragrant flowers it is an attractive (climbing) plant for indoors and out of doors. Indoors, jasmin is often trained along a trellis or iron hoops. This woody plant has climbing stems and twining shoots, or long, thin twigs with single or compound leaves in pairs or spreading, and white, pinkish-red or yellow clusters of flowers with a wonderful fragrance, the petals of which form a long, narrow tube.
J. meysni (syn. *J. primulinum*) is an evergreen covered in leaves, with squarish, slightly twining green stems, and compound leaves consisting of lanceolate leaflets. It has bright yellow flowers, 3-5 cm in diameter, which grow separately and are not fragrant. When it is trained, the plant can grow more than 2 m high.
J. officinale, white jasmine, is a climber up to 4 m tall, which loses its leaves. It has compound, much divided leaves, a long,

Jathropha

60   3-10

Jathropha was originally indigenous in tropical regions of Asia and Africa, and is nowadays found growing wild throughout the tropics. There are approximately 170 species, including various succulents. *J. podagrica*, with its striking appearance, is especially cultivated as a house plant. *J. podagrica* has a succulent, bottle-like, branching stem which serves as a water reservoir. The neck of the bottle branches out at the top, and there are long-stemmed, large, shield-shaped, irregularly lobed, slightly indented leaves, and orange or bright red flowerheads also on long stems. This plant requires a warm, sunny spot and nutritious, porous soil, e.g., a mixture of leaf-mould and clay. During the growing period (March to September/October), water sparingly, adding some plant food once a month (not too much, or the plant will lose its shape). 20-24° C. During the resting period the leaves drop off; place in a light, cooler spot (16° C), almost dry, and gradually start giving more water as the growing tips appear. When the plant is laid horizontally after the resting period, new growing tips can also develop from the thickened base. Repot every year in spring, keeping the soil fairly dry (for recovery of roots). Propagate from seed. (After artificial pollination the dispersed seeds must be collected.)

Justicia

 50-100 ○ ⊗ 6-9 ! ⊽ ⊠

Justicia is found in temperate and subtropical regions throughout the world. It now also comprises species formerly classified under the genus *Jacobinia*, including *J. carnea*, formerly known as *Jacobinia carnea*, the species which is cultivated most commonly as a house plant. This is a herbaceous plant or (semi-)shrub with undivided pairs of leaves, and two-lipped, partly tubular, red, purple, yellow or white flowers.
J. carnea (syn. *Jacobinia carnea, Jacobinia magnifica*), King's Crown, is indigenous in Brazil, where the shrub grows to a height of 150-200 cm (indoors, it grows to a height of approximately 100 cm). It grows quickly, and has erect stems with long-stemmed, large, oval, pointed leaves with deep veins, and striking, compact, broad, plume-like flowerheads, 10 cm long, consisting of long, narrow, two-lipped, salmon or purplish-red flowers with green or purplish bracts.
This plant requires a warm, very light spot protected against bright sunlight, and good potting compost mixed with some clay or loam. Temperature 20-22° C during the growing period. Water liberally and spray with tepid water (not on the flowers). The plant can be placed on an upturned saucer in a dish of water. Feed once a week. During the resting period (autumn/winter) place in a cooler spot (13-16° C), water less, and do not feed. It is normal for some leaves to drop off. Prune back hard in spring (flowers bloom on young shoots). Repot if necessary in a pot which is not too large. If the plant wilts, the soil is too dry. Propagate from young stem cuttings (spring).

Jathropha podagrica

Justicia carnea

49

Kalanchoë

Kalanchoë

Kalanchoë

○ ↕ 20-30 ○ ✿ available all year round ⎁

Kalanchoë is indigenous in Africa, Asia and on Madagascar. It comprises more than 200 species, varying from plants which are 10 cm tall to shrubs, climbers and trees 10 m tall. By artificially extending daylight hours the varieties cultivated as house plants are available all year round; after flowering they are usually discarded.

This is a succulent with thick, fleshy pairs or rosettes of undivided leaves, usually with serrated margins, and erect or pendent plumes or clusters consisting of four flowers. *K. blossfeldiana*, "Flaming Katy", has shiny, green, oval leaves, with a reddish, coarsely serrated margin and short-stemmed, light red clusters of flowers. It is the parent plant of many hybrids, including "Bali", orange red; "Beta", yellow; "Bingo", purple; "Burrasca", white; "Forty-niner", yellow; "Hurricane", red; "Mistral", lilac; "Tarantella", orange.

Kalanchoë "Tessa" flowers profusely with pendent, narrow, lantern-shaped orange flowers. It can also be placed outside in a sheltered, sunny position; "Wendy" has

thick, erect stems and fairly large, pendent,
balloon-like, pinky-red flowers.
This plant requires a sunny, warm spot,
16-22° C. Keep fairly moist and feed once
every two weeks. Remove blooms after
flowering. The plant can flower for several
months, and is then discarded. Propagate
from top or leaf cuttings, preferably in
spring.

Kohleria

○ ↕ 20-60 ◐ ✿ 7-8 ▽

Kohleria is indigenous in Mexico and the
north of South America. The main house
plants available are hybrids of *K. amabilis*,
K. bogotensis and *K. eriantha*.
This is a herbaceous plant with scaly
rhizomes which grow underground, and
hairy, slightly woody stems with soft,
velvety pairs of leaves and flowers which
grow on their own or in groups in the leaf
axilla or at the end of the stems. They
consist of five very hairy petals, which have
largely fused to form a rather rounded tube,
ending in five spreading lobes which are
white, yellow, orange, pink, red or violet,
often with beautiful markings or lines.
K. amabilis has rather limp stems up to
60 cm long, with large, dark green, broad,
oval leaves with purplish-brown veins, and
bright pink flowers with purplish-red spots,
growing on their own or in pairs in the leaf
axilla; hybrids do not grow as tall and have
plain leaves.
K. bogotensis has sturdier stems with green
or brownish-green oval leaves with light
green veins, and pendent flowers on stems,
consisting of red petals forming a tube, with
a white or light yellow mouth dotted with
red. Hybrids have plain green leaves and
less striking markings.
K. eriantha, up to 120 cm tall (hybrids,
20-45 cm tall), has long, white or red hairy
stems with thick, large oval leaves and red
hairy margins. Usually the long-stemmed,
orangey-red flowers spotted with yellow
grow in groups of three or four together.
Hybrids have broader and more striking
mouths.
This plant requires a warm, light spot
protected against sunlight and extra acid,

Kohleria

well-drained, airy soil, e.g., a mixture of
leaf-mould, peat and perlite. During the
growing season, water moderately with soft,
tepid water, and feed every two or three
weeks (half concentration). For high
humidity, place plant on an upturned saucer
in a dish of water. 18-25° C. Support
drooping stems. Water less after flowering
and place in a cool, light spot in winter
(12-15° C). Prune back every year. Propagate
by dividing rhizome or from top cuttings in
autumn for early flowering, or from seed
(January) for late flowering.

Mandevilla

⛅ ↕ 30-50 ○ ◉ ✿ 4-9 ! 🪣 ✂

Mandevilla, indigenous from Argentina to Mexico, is still often sold under the well-known synonym, *Dipladenia*.

This evergreen, climbing shrub grows up to 4 m tall and has pairs or whorls of leaves, and trumpet-shaped, white, pink or purple flowers which grow in clusters in the leaf axilla or at the end of the stem. The calyx consists of five spreading, elegantly undulating petals.

M. boliviensis (syn. *Dipladenia boliviensis*) has pairs of long-stemmed, oval, pointed leaves and beautiful clusters of rather vulnerable, fragrant, white flowers 5 cm across, which grow in the leaf axilla.

M. sanderi (syn. *Dipladenia sanderi*) is a strong climbing plant with pairs of short-stemmed, broad, oval leaves, and beautiful, yellow-throated pink flowers, 7 cm across; "Rosea" has pale pink to salmon-coloured flowers with a yellow throat.

M. splendens (syn. *Dipladenia splendens*) has smooth stems and fairly short-stemmed, thin, broad, oval, slightly hairy leaves, and clusters of large, pinky-red flowers, 8-10 cm across, which grow in the leaf axilla.

M. x amabilis (syn. *Dipladenia x amabilis*) flowers profusely and has broad, oval pointed leaves and pink or red flowers 8 cm across; "Amoena" has bright pink, yellow-throated flowers; "Rubiniana" has dark pink flowers.

This plant requires a warm light spot, protected from bright sunlight, and nutritious, well-drained soil, e.g., a mixture of leaf-mould, clay, sharp sand, peat and old cow manure. During the growing period water liberally and spray with tepid water. Feed once a week. 18-24° C, and high humidity. During the resting period (autumn to March), place in a cooler spot (1315° C), water less, do not feed, and prune back before new growth begins. Repot every year in March. Propagate from cuttings (June/July) using a rooting hormone. The young plants should be cultivated in a heated greenhouse.

Mandevilla x amabilis
"Rubiuiana"

Mandevilla sanderia
(Dipladenia)

Medinilla

○ ↕ 70-100 ⊘ ✿ 2/3-8 ⊞ ⬕

Medinilla is indigenous in tropical regions of West Africa and Asia. It comprises approximately 400 epiphytic species, but only *M. magnifica* is cultivated.

This beautiful plant requires high humidity and is not particularly suitable as a house plant, though it is ideal for a conservatory or greenhouse.

M. magnifica can grow to a height of 2.5 m in the Philippines. The cultivar grows up to 1 m tall, a broad, branching shrub with short, woody trunks and thick, squarish branches with large leathery pairs of dark green, yellow-veined leaves, and long, pendent flowering stems with large, pink flowerheads, consisting of many small clustered florets and one or two rings of pale pink bracts.

This plant requires a warm, light spot protected from bright sunlight, and nutritious soil, e.g., a mixture of crumbly clay, leaf-mould, sharp sand and cow manure. Water moderately in summer. Immerse occasionally, and regularly spray leaves with soft, tepid water. Feed every other week until the end of August. Ensure that there is plenty of fresh air. 18-22° C. For high humidity, place plant on an upturned saucer in a dish of water. During the important resting period (from November), place in a cooler spot (14-16° C) with less or almost no water. As soon as the buds appear, gradually increase water and place in a warmer spot. Repot in spring, and prune back if necessary. Propagate from top cuttings.

Medinilla

Medinilla maginifica

Neoregelia
Bird's nest bromeliad

○ ↑ 25 ⊘ ✿ available all year round 🏺 ✂

Neoregelia is mainly indigenous in Brazil. The genus comprises about 40 epiphytic species. The rather plain lilac flowers at the base of the rosette of leaves are surrounded by brightly coloured inner leaves. The plant is usually sold when it is due to flower; after flowering, the rosette dies off and the plant is often discarded. New plants which flower after two to three years can be obtained from offsets. The rosette of shiny, sword-like or tongue-shaped, serrated shiny pointed leaves form a central cup or vase. The outer leaves are dark green or variegated, surrounding the bright red, brownish-red, purple or lilac "bird's nest".
N. carolinae has spreading, shiny green leaves, 40 cm long and 5 cm wide, and the inner leaves are bright red, surrounding the violet flowers up to 5 cm tall; "Flandria" has green leaves with yellowish-white serrated margins; "Meyendorffii", has a funnel-shaped rosette of olive-green leaves; "Tricolor Perfecta" has splendid, yellowish-green leaves with stripes running lengthways.
N. concentrica has broad, brown, spiny leaves, 30 cm long. The inner leaves are a purplish lilac and the flowers are light blue. This plant requires a cool, light spot protected from bright sunlight, and lime-free soil, rich in humus, e.g., a mixture of rotted leaves, old cow manure and sphagnum moss, moderately moist. The central cup should always be full of lime-free water, even when the plant is flowering, but empty and rinse it from time to time. Add liquid plant food every other week (also in the cup). Placing the plant in a cool spot (12-15° C) delays the dying process. At a fairly late stage, cut off the offsets from the old rosette when they have taken root, and cultivate in a nursery

Neoregelia,
Bird's nest bromeliad

greenhouse. Also propagate from runners
(variegated varieties) and from seed.

Nertera
Coral moss

○ ↕ 5-15 ◉ ✿ 3-5 ✤ 4-8 ▯ ⋉

Nertera is indigenous in mountain regions
of the southern hemisphere. It comprises
12 low-growing, clump-forming species, of
which only *N. granadensis* is cultivated.
Its ornamental value is determined by the
berry-like fruits which often remain on the
plant for a long time.
N. granadensis has creeping, leafy stems with
pairs of oval, blunt leaves, 4-8 mm long,
and unremarkable green flowers, followed

by bright orange berries up to 8 mm in
diameter.
This plant requires a fairly light spot,
protected from bright sunlight, and soil rich
in humus, e.g., a mixture of leaf-mould, old
cow manure and some clay. In summer,
water regularly with soft water in a dish (to
prevent rotting). Ensure plenty of fresh air.
Feed every other week. Water less in winter.
Repot if necessary in spring. Propagate from
seed (February/March) and by dividing
plants (August).

*Nertera granadensis,
Coral moss*

Pachystachys

🌿 ⬍ 50-75 ◯ ✤ 3-10 🪣

Pachystachys is indigenous in tropical regions of America and in the West Indies. There are five species, of which *P. lutea* has been cultivated since 1900. Its popularity has fluctuated, but recently it has again been very popular. It is a shrub-like plant with erect, compact flowerheads of red or white flowers which quickly drop off, and green or yellow bracts which remain on the plant for a long time.

P. lutea, the lollipop plant, flowers profusely. This semi-shrub grows to a height of 1-2 m (cultivated variety, up to 75 cm). It has dark green, lanceolate, pointed, deeply veined leaves, and erect flowerheads, consisting of bright yellow (reversed) overlapping bracts and (yellowish) white flowers.

This plant requires a warm, very light spot with high humidity, and nutritious (standard) potting compost. During the growing period, keep moderately moist, and feed every two weeks. For high humidity, spray regularly and place the plant on an upturned saucer in a dish of water.

18-24° C. A lot of light promotes strong, compact growth and beautifully coloured bracts. During the resting period (winter), place in a cooler spot (min. 15° C) and keep dry. In spring, prune back hard and repot. Flowerheads which drop off after purchase because of a change in the environment are quickly replaced by new ones, if the plant is properly cared for. Propagate from cuttings (spring). This is fairly easy using rooting powder. Pinch out tips of young plants several times for bushy growth.

Pachystachys lutea

Passiflora
Passion flower

○ ↕ 30-50 (tied up) ○ ✿ 3-9 🏺 ✂

The shape of the flowers of *Passiflora*, which is indigenous in tropical and subtropical areas of America and Asia, is sometimes related to the suffering of Christ (the Passion) as follows: the ten petals represent the ten good apostles (without Judas, who betrayed Christ, and Peter, who denied Him), or the Ten Commandments; the three-coloured ring of numerous filaments is the Crown of Thorns or halo; the colours purple, white and brown, refer to various garments; the five stamens to the five wounds. As a house plant it is often trained along iron hoops.

This is a woody climber with tendrils spiralling from the axilla, which twine around leaves, stems and branches.

The shoots are stiff at first and flexible later on. The large flowers open at different times of the day and usually flower for only one day. *P. caerulea* is a climbing plant, 6-9 m long (Peru), with a light green deeply indented, broad, heart-shaped leaf, lanceolate petals and single, slightly fragrant, white flowers, 7-10 cm across, with a blue ring of ray flowers and purple styles. There are several cultivars, such as "Victoria", which has lilac and white flowers. It can also be grown outside in a sunny spot, protected from frost.

This plant requires a sunny spot and ordinary potting compost with loam.
Keep moist at all times in the summer. Feed once a week. 15-20° C (no warmer). Train the plant around the iron hoop, or along a window frame. Keep cooler in winter (10-15° C) and reduce watering. The leaves fall off. If necessary, repot in spring and prune back hard. Propagate by removing runners from roots and from top cuttings.

top and bottom: Passiflora, Passion flower

57

Pelargonium,
Geranium

Pelargonium
Geranium

○ | ↕ 25-80 ○ ❀ 3/4-8 ▯ ◁

Pelargonium is mainly indigenous in South Africa. The name is derived from the Greek word, "pelargos" (stork), which refers to the shape of the fruit which looks rather like the long, pointed beak of a stork. It is also popularly known as geranium, which can lead to confusion with the related genus, *Geranium* (stork's beak). There are about 250 *Pelargonium* species and thousands of hybrids, which are still increasing in number. A number of species produce profusely flowering house plants, including the well-known *zonal, peltatum* and *grandiflorum* hybrids.

This is an annual or perennial, herbaceous, sometimes rather woody plant, with long-stemmed, spreading, usually indented leaves, sometimes fragrant, and clusters of flowers.

P. grandiflorum hybrids (parent plants include *P. grandiflorum* and *P. cucullatum,*

Pelargonium
"Hollywood star",
Geranium

Pelargonium x Argonium x Domesticum hybrids, Geranium

French geranium, have sturdy, erect, hairless stems and green, serrated leaves, which are not fragrant. The profuse blooms consist of large, red, orange, pink, salmon, violet, lilac and white flowers with dark markings.

P. peltatum hybrids (crossed from *P. peltatum* and *P. hederifolium* etc.) are hanging geraniums with thin, hanging or creeping stems, shiny, green decorative leaves, and red, pink, salmon, lilac, white or bicoloured flowers, either single or double. These plants are very suitable for growing on balconies.

P. zonal hybrids (crossed from *P. zonale* and *P. inquinans* etc.) have thick, fleshy, hairy, erect stems, virtually round leaves which are scented when they are bruised, and have broad, brown markings or a zone on the upper side in a colour which varies for each variety. The single and double flowers come in every shade of red, orange, salmon, pink, lilac and white. The compact, profusely flowering varieties are particularly suitable for growing indoors.

Species which are particularly popular for their fragrance include *P. crispum* (syn. *P. x citrosum*), lemon geranium, which has branching stems with short-stemmed, heart-shaped, frizzy, lobed leaves which smell of lemon, and pink, dark-veined flowers; *P. graveolens*, the rose geranium, has felty, hairy, bluish-green, deeply indented, palmate, lobed leaves, which smell of roses, and white or lilac flowers with burgundy spots; *P. radens* has palmate, fragrant leaves, narrow pinnate leaflets, and short-stemmed pink, dark-veined clusters of flowers.

This plant requires a light, sunny spot and well-drained, standard potting compost with some sharp sand and clay. During the flowering period, water with tepid water; alternately water the compost and saucer. Mist in the evening. 15-30° C. Cooler during the resting period, 8-10° C, and keep fairly dry, but not quite dried out.

Turn plants regularly for a good shape. Only break off blooms which have finished flowering, and not the flowering stem, which will drop off of its own accord. Repot annually (spring). Propagation is fairly easy from top cuttings.

Plumbago

 30-50 ⊘ ✿ 5-9 ⊟ ⊠

The sap of *Plumbago*, which is indigenous in tropical and subtropical regions throughout the world, is said to turn the skin a leaden colour.

This climber has long, twining stems, spreading leaves and blue, white or red flowers with five sepals and a small tube consisting of five spreading, circular petals. As a house plant, it is often trained along iron hoops.

P. auriculata (syn. *P. capensis*), Cape Leadwort, first has erect, and later twining, long green stems with short-stemmed narrow or oval leaves. The underside of the leaves and stems are covered with white scales. The plant has beautiful clusters of hairy blooms, consisting of large numbers of sky-blue flowers; "Alba" has white flowers.

P. indica (syn. *P. rosea*) has thin stems and slender, racemes of pinky-red blooms. It requires more heat.

This plant requires a light spot protected from bright sunlight, and nutritious, well-drained soil, e.g., a mixture of leaf-mould, clay or loam, and old cow manure. Water liberally during the growing season and feed every two weeks. 15-25° C, cooler in winter (7-14° C), *P. indica*, minimum 13° C. Place in a light spot, water sparingly, though the soil should not dry out. Prune back in spring and remove stems which have finished flowering. Repot in spring. Propagate from (semi-woody) top cuttings (summer).

Primula
Primrose

• ○ ⫯ 15-30 ⊘ ✿ available all year round

! ⊟ ⊟

Primula is mainly indigenous in mountainous regions in the northern hemisphere. The genus comprises about 500 species, of which only a few are cultivated

*Plumbago auriculata
"Alba"*

as house plants, although there are countless hybrids on offer. The plants flower profusely, but are often difficult to keep, and are therefore discarded after flowering. This is an annual or biennial plant with single, lobed or serrated leaves in rings or rosettes, and large trumpet-shaped flowers, often with stems, growing in groups of five. They consist of a tubular serrated throat, a long tube-shaped corolla, and spreading petals in many shades of white, yellow, orange, pink, red, purple, violet and blue.
P. x kewensis, a hybrid of *P. floribunda* and *P. verticillata*, has pale green spatulate leaves, often covered with white powder, and large yellow flowers which are arranged in tiers and flower from February to April.
P. malacoides, fairy primrose, an annual plant, has compact rosettes of leaves covered with white powder, and stems and flower stalks in steps on the main stalk, and white, pale pink or red flowers with a yellow centre. Many varieties are not powdery. This plant flowers from January to March.
P. obconica, poison primrose, is a perennial plant with pale green, hairy, oval, coarsely serrated leaves and crimson, pink, blue, white, or salmon-orange blooms which flower in stages. The plant secretes primuline, which produces an itchy rash in some people, though there are varieties available that do not do this. These plants originally flowered in June/July; cultivars flower for a few months.
P. praenitens (syn. *P. sinensis*), the Chinese primula, is an annual plant which forms rosettes of slightly hairy, deeply lobed, serrated leaves, and has long-stemmed, sometimes tiered clusters of large white, orange or red flowers, often with indented petals.
P. vulgaris hybrids (syn. *P. acaulis*) are perennial plants which form rosettes and have sulphur yellow flowers without stems. A process of selection has resulted in a large variety of colours and sizes, and there are also double and even long-stemmed varieties. To prolong flowering as long as possible, place the plant in a cool, light spot, protected from bright sunlight. 10-15° C. Water liberally with soft water, and add plant food every two weeks (half concentration). Do not spray the leaves. After flowering, the plant is usually discarded, although the perennial varieties can be put outside in the garden. Propagate from seed (June/July).

Primula obconica, Primrose

Primula obconica hybrids, Primrose

Rhododendron simsii,
Azalea

Rhododendron
Azalea

⚘ ↕ 30-50 ◐ ✿ various 🪣 ✂

Rhododendron is found throughout the world, but is not indigenous in Africa and South America. For some time the house plants and garden plants classified under *Azalea* in the past have now been included in this genus. Some important species for growing indoors include *R. simsii* and *R. obtusum*, which come from China and Japan. They were at the beginning of the range, which is still expanding. This is an evergreen or deciduous shrub with

spreading, smooth-edged leaves, often arranged in rings, and flowers which sometimes grow singly, usually at the ends of the stem or sometimes in the leaf axilla. They have five to ten irregular petals in a bell, trumpet, tube, beaker or dish shape, in every possible colour. *R. obtusum*, Japanese azalea, is virtually winter-hardy, but loses some of its leaves. It is a branching shrub with shiny, dark green, oval blunt leaves, and pink, orange or bright red, single or double flowers, 2-3 cm across in groups of 2 to 5. The so-called *amoena* hybrids were produced by crossing *R. kaempferi* and *R. kiusianum*. These come in many different shades and are also suitable for the garden. *R. simsii* (syn. *Azalea indica*, the Indian azalea) is not winter-hardy. It has dark green leaves with thick coarse hair on the underside, and single or double flowers 5 cm across, in every shade of white, pink, violet, red and orange. It is fairly easy to force hybrids to flower, and after flowering they are often discarded as it is difficult to keep the plant. Early flowering varieties (from October) include "Aline", white; "Ambrosiana", dark red; "Bertina", pink; "Flamingo", purple; "Inga", pink with white margins; "Kosmos", purplish-pink; "Osta", white with a red heart; medium and late flowering varieties (from January/February) include "Adonia", dark red/purple; "Friedhelm Scherrer", orangey-red; "Glaser", orange; "Gloria", pink; "Knut Erwen", pinkish-red; "Leopold Astrid", pinkish-red with white spots; "Price", bright red; "Rosali", bright pink; "Stella Maris", white with pale pink markings. Varieties such as "Helmut Vogel", dark red, are sold all year round.

Rhododendron simsii,
Azalea

To flower for a long time, this plant requires a cool light spot, out of the sun, and well-drained, lime-free soil, e.g., coniferous woodland soil, peat and old cow manure. Keep moist at all times and water liberally with lime-free (rain) water during the flowering period. Immerse once a week and do not feed. The plant is very sensitive to salt. Only spray leaves (the flowers suffer from watering). After flowering, the Japanese azalea can be planted in the garden in a sheltered, light spot. Of the other indoor azaleas, plants which flower in February/March have the best chance of surviving. After flowering, remove dead blooms with stems, repot the plant and place in a light spot in a cooler position (6-10° C). Remove first shoots, keep soil moist and immerse plants weekly until July/August. Feed occasionally and place in a warm position when the buds start to swell. Repot a few weeks after flowering. Propagate from cuttings (February/April or August/September).

Rosa

Miniature rose

 15-40 several times

Rosa, Miniature rose

Rosa is indigenous in the temperate regions of the northern hemisphere. It is undoubtedly the best known and most popular garden plant. A number of dwarf varieties have been cultivated by crossing species such as *R. chinensis* "Minima". These do not grow too large and can flower several times in a sunny spot. Miniature roses are low-growing (15-30 cm), woody stemmed shrubs, sometimes with spiny stems and compound leaves, consisting of three or five leaflets, and small flowers in many shades of red, pink, yellow, orange, violet and white. The plants are sold under the name of the particular variety. They are propagated from cuttings and are available all year round thanks to the use of artificial lighting. "Rosamini" roses can also be placed outside. These include "Amanda", which has dark red flowers; "Amorette", white; "Bluenette", violet-pink; "Finstar", orangey-pink; "Guletta", yellow; "Red Minimo", dark red. "Meillandina" roses are not winter-hardy. These include "Apricot", which is an apricot colour; "Duke", pink; "Golden", yellow; "Lady", pink; "Sunny", yellow. This plant requires a sunny, light spot and special potting compost. Water liberally and feed once a week. After flowering, prune back to half the height for a second flowering (approximately six weeks later). In the garden, they need the same treatment as outdoor roses. Repot if necessary in special potting compost. Propagate from seed and from cuttings.

Rosa

63

Saintpaulia,
African violet

Senecio,
Cape ivy

Saintpaulia
African violet

○ | ↕ 10-20 ⊘ ✿ all year round ▱

Saintpaulia is indigenous in tropical rainforests in East Africa. It comprises about 20 species. The popular house plants are hybrids of *S. ionantha* and *S. confusa.* They can be kept for years, and with the help of a lamp, they will flower almost all year round. There is an enormous range. Originally there were many American varieties, but nowadays there are more German and French varieties. This is a fairly flat, hairy plant with virtually no stalk, usually forming rosettes. The fleshy leaves have long stems, and there are groups of two to eight long-stemmed, violet-blue flowers consisting of five petals with yellow anthers. *S. ionantha* hybrids are pot plants which flower profusely all year round. There are single and double varieties in shades of blue, pink, salmon, lilac, purple and white, or bicoloured, with smooth-edged or frizzy petals. The "Mini" hybrids are becoming increasingly popular. This plant requires a light spot which is not too sunny (east-facing window) and nutritious potting compost with peat, which is poor in lime. The soil should not be too moist, but should be fairly dry. Water moderately with soft, tepid water (cold water produces yellow spots), and feed once a week. 18-20° C. Do not place in the warm air currents of central heating. If the humidity is low, place on an upturned saucer in a dish of water. It is advisable for the plant to

have a resting period once a year in a cooler spot (16 ° C) with less water. Then it can be repotted. Repot annually in spring in shallow, broad pots. Propagate fairly easily from leaf cuttings (August/September).

Senecio
Cape ivy

• | ↕ 20-30 ⊘ ✿ all year round ! ▱ ✄

Senecio is a very large genus, comprising approximately 1,300 species. It is found throughout the world, and there are annual, biennial and perennial herbaceous and woody stemmed or succulent varieties. Hybrids of, for example, *S. cruentus* and *S. maderensis* are cultivated as annuals with attractive flowers. When they stand in a draught, they are extremely sensitive to aphids. They are also known by the name cineraria. *S. cruentus* (syn. *Cineraria cruenta*) is a herbaceous annual, with large, broad, hairy, irregularly indented and slightly lobed leaves, which are green on the upper side, and pale green or purplish underneath. The broad, compact clusters of flowers grow at the end of the stems and consist of a large number of flowerheads up to 8 cm across, in every shade of blue, purplish-red, pink, terracotta and white. They can also be bicoloured, sometimes spotted, and are single or double. The small-flowered "Multiflora" varieties

have the most attractive flowers.
This plant requires a cool, light,
draught-free spot. Water moderately with
tepid water. Spray occasionally and feed
once a week. If it is too warm the plant will
soon finish flowering. It is sensitive to too
much water, and the leaves will wilt and
not recover. (If the leaves wilt because it is
too dry, they will recover.) After flowering
(3-4 weeks), the plant is discarded.
Propagate from seed (this is difficult).

Sinningia
Gloxinia

⚬ ⬆ 20-30 ◷ ❀ 4-8 ⚠ 🪣

The genus *Sinningia*, which is indigenous in
Brazil, has for some time also included a
number of Reichsteineria species, including
the well-known cardinal flower, as well as
a number of *Gloxinia* species, which has led
to some confusion about the name. It is
a herbaceous, extremely hairy plant, with a
tuber which grows below the ground, pairs
of oval serrated leaves and short-stemmed,
tubular or bell-shaped flowers which grow
on their own or in groups in the leaf axilla.
S. cardinalis (syn. *Reichsteineria cardinalis*,
Gesneria cardinalis), Cardinal flower, has
very hairy stems, bright green, broad oval
leaves covered with pale green hair, and
horizontally spreading, tubular, lip-shaped
red flowers 5 cm long, in plumes. There is
also a variety with white flowers.
S. x hybrida, parentage includes *S. speciosa*
(syn. *Gloriosa speciosa*) and *S. regina*,
Gloxinia, has large, velvety, hairy, dark
green oval leaves without stems, and
long-stemmed, large, bell-shaped, red and
white, white, purple, spotted, double
flowers which usually grow on their own.
This plant requires a warm, light, shady
spot and nutritious soil poor in lime, e.g.,
a mixture of leaf-mould, peat and old cow
manure. Water liberally with soft tepid
water, and feed once a week. Remove
blooms when they have finished flowering
from the base, but continue feeding the
plants when they have finished flowering
(until September/October). Then water less.
Allow the leaves to die off, and store the
tuber in a dry place at 15-18° C. Do not
allow the soil to dry out completely. When
new shoots appear (end of February),
remove the old earth from the tuber and
replant hollow side up. Keep warm (20° C),
and water moderately, adding plant food
after 5/6 weeks. Propagate from leaf
cuttings and runners, or by dividing the
tuber.

*Sinningia speciosa "Gerda Lodden",
Gloxinia*

*Sinningia "Diego",
Gloxinia*

65

Spathiphyllum cannifolium

Spathiphyllum

 30-70 3-4

Spathiphyllum is mainly indigenous in tropical regions of America. At first sight it is very similar to *Anthurium*, but closer inspection shows that the leaves and flowers have a different shape.

This is an evergreen marsh plant which forms clumps. It has long-stemmed, dark green, lanceolate or long, oval, usually spreading leaves, and an erect inflorescence consisting of a spadix covered with small florets, and a white or greenish spathe. Current varieties are hybrids of, e.g., S. *cochlearispathum*, which has lanceolate, wavy leaves, and a hollow, lanceolate or oval, white spathe, 30 cm long, and S. *wallisii*, the Peace lily, which has shiny, long, lanceolate, wavy leaves, a reed-like stem, and a hollow, oval, white spathe which turns green. The range is fairly large and is still expanding, partly as the result of in vitro fertilization. The plants can have one or several, often long-stemmed flowers, magnificent white spathes with a white spadix with a green stem.

This plant requires a warm, light spot, protected from sunlight, and well-drained soil, rich in humus, e.g., a mixture of peat, leaf-mould, clay and old cow manure. Keep moist and water liberally with tepid water during the growing period. Spray regularly, and feed every other week. High humidity. 18-24° C. Keep slightly cooler during the resting period (16-18° C) and water moderately. Brown spots mean that the plant has had too much plant food or salt, and should be repotted. Repot every two or three years (late in winter/early in spring). Propagate by dividing and from seed.

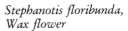

Stephanotis floribunda,
Wax flower

Stephanotis
Wax flower

Stephanotis is indigenous in Madagascar. The only species to be cultivated is *S. floribunda*. It is not an easy plant to cultivate, though it is strong, and with proper care, the beautifully fragrant flowers return every year. It is usually trained along iron hoops. With the proper lighting and temperature it is available in flower all year round. *S. floribunda* is often associated with bridal bouquets. It is an evergreen climber with tough, twining stems several metres long, shiny, dark green oval leaves, and prolific umbels of fragrant, tubular white flowers which grow in the leaf axilla, and consist of five spreading, star-shaped perianth lobes. This plant requires a warm, light spot, protected from the sun (east-facing window), and nutritious soil, rich in humus, e.g., a mixture of leaf-mould, sharp sand, clay and old cow manure. Keep moderately moist; the soil should not dry out. During the growing season (summer), water liberally with soft tepid (rain) water. Spray leaves occasionally and feed every other week. 18-24° C. Keep cooler during the resting period in winter (12-14° C), water sparingly, so that the soil is slightly moist, and do not feed. The plant is sensitive to large fluctuations in temperature. After purchase the buds may fall off because the light comes from a different direction. It should always be facing the light on the same side (put a mark on the pot). Always train the new stems around the hoops so that the plant can be moved. The buds start to form at the end of the winter and the plants can flower earlier with artificial lighting. Repot every year (spring). Propagate from cuttings of old shoots (spring/summer), using a rooting powder.

Streptocarpus,
Cape primrose

Streptocarpus
Cape primrose

○ ↕ 15-60 ✿ ❋ 5-10 🥛

Streptocarpus is mainly indigenous in tropical rainforests in South Africa and Madagascar, and comprises over 100 annual and perennial species. A process of selection and hybridization has produced a large range of strong, attractive house plants which is still expanding.
This is a herbaceous plant, sometimes with stemless, large and fragile rosettes of leaves in groups, though sometimes there is only one leaf, or stems with pairs of leaves.
The leafless flowering stalk has one or more blue, pinkish-red, red or white flowers, consisting of five small sepals and a long corolla, composed of five spreading, round, uneven lobed petals.
Streptocarpus hybrids are crossed mainly from *S. dunnii*, which usually has one rather large, coarsely serrated leaf, and flowering stalks with many trumpet-shaped, pinkish-red or red flowers, several of which open at the same time; *S. parviflorus*, a smaller species, which forms rosettes of strap-shaped, round, serrated leaves, and has many white trumpet-shaped flowers with a stripy throat which open at the same time; *S. polyanthus*, which has broad, oval, light or greyish-green serrated leaves, (greenish) white or pale lilac flowers; *S. rexii*, which has many short, hairy, strap-shaped, blunt serrated leaves and one to six lilac-white flowers, striped with violet on every flowering stalk. In addition to the varieties with large flowers, there are also varieties which flower profusely with small flowers in many colours. *S. wendlandii* has a large fragile leaf and a plume-like inflorescence

up to 7 cm long with a large number of small blue flowers.
This plant requires a warm, light spot protected from the sun (east or west-facing window), and standard potting compost. Keep moderately moist, water regularly with tepid water during the growing season (not on the leaves) and feed every other week. For high humidity place the plant on an upturned saucer in a dish of water. 18-24° C. Remove old leaves and flowers with the stalk. During the resting period (winter), keep cooler (12-15° C) and drier. Repot every year after the resting period (spring). Propagate from leaf cuttings (cut the leaf along the central vein and place the cut edge in moist peat).

Thunbergia
Black-eyed Susan

● ○ ↕ 50-80 ○ ❋ 3-9 🥛 🥛

Thunbergia is indigenous in Central and South America, Asia and Madagascar. It comprises about 200 species, of which *T. alata*, Black-eyed Susan, is particularly popular. It is generally cultivated as an annual plant, and trained along a trellis or hoops.
This is an annual or perennial woody or herbaceous plant with pairs of leaves and striking blue, yellow, orange or white flowers which usually grow on their own, and have a large, trumpet-like corolla, consisting of five petals.
T. alata is a perennial climbing plant, cultivated as an annual, with triangular, oval, serrated leaves, twining stems and bright orange flowers with a black eye; "Alba" has white flowers with a dark eye. *T. fragrans* is a perennial climbing plant with woody stems, and shiny, green, triangular, long oval leaves on stems. It has single, fragrant white flowers.
This plant requires a draught-free, sunny spot. Water regularly and feed once a week. 18-25° C. *T. alata* usually dies off after flowering and is discarded. *T. fragrans* can be kept on the windowsill; repot if necessary. Propagate from seed in shallow trays (spring).

Triplochlamys

🌿 ⬍ 50-100 ◯ ◐ ✿ all year round ▽

Triplochlamys is indigenous in tropical regions in South America. It comprises five species, of which only one is cultivated, viz., *T. multiflora*, which in the past was classified under *Pavonia*. A process of selection has produced strong plants which flower throughout the year.

This is an evergreen shrub with spreading, stemmed, long, smooth-edged or serrated leaves and supporting leaves at the base of the stem. It has pinkish-red or purple flowers with a collar of five or more linear bracts below the calyx.

T. multiflora (syn. *Pavonia multiflora, P. rosea*) has slightly hairy, pale or dark green, slightly serrated leaves. The purplish-red flowers grow on their own in the axilla of the upper leaves. They have a bright red calyx and purple, rolled-up petals which do not spread. This plant requires a light spot, protected from bright sunlight, and standard potting compost, rich in humus. Keep moist at all times, water liberally and immerse when leaves are limp. Feed once a week (spring to autumn). In winter, minimum 12° C. If the plant does not have a resting period in winter (in a cooler spot with less water), it becomes ugly after two to three years. Prune back (in spring) to 20-30 cm, and place in a cooler spot for some time. Repot every year in spring. Propagate from top cuttings, using rooting powder (spring).

Thunbergia alata,
Black-eyed Susan

Triplochlamys multiflora

Vriesea "Christiane"

Vriesea

⬭ ↕ 30-190 ◯ ◑ ✿ 5-10 ⬚ ⊰

Vriesea is indigenous in Central and South America. It comprises about 250, mostly epiphytic species, of which a large number are cultivated. There are also many hybrids available.

This plant has large, funnel-shaped rosettes of beautiful, long, thin, smooth-edged leaves, often with markings, and a striking, colourful flowerhead. After flowering for a long time the rosette dies off and new plants can be cultivated from the young shoots.

V. carinata has a cylindrical rosette of broad, pale green, tongue-shaped leaves, and an unbranching red stem, 15-30 cm long, with yellow flowers with a green tip and bracts which are red at the base and yellow at the tips, flecked with green.

V. fenestralis has a pale green rosette of leaves with dark green stripes and purple spots on the underside, and an unbranching stem, 30-75 cm long, with yellowish-white flowers and green bracts.

V. hieroglyphica has a large rosettes of leaves, 100-150 cm in diameter. The leaves are green, 60-90 cm long and 5-12 cm wide, with dark green markings on the upper side, and almost black on the underside. It has a branching stem, 120-180 cm long, and yellow flowers with pale green bracts. Cultivars rarely flower.

V. x poelmannii has pale green leaves, a large, (un)branched flowering spike, yellow flowers and crimson bracts with yellowish-green tips.

V. splendens, Flaming sword, has slightly arching, bright green leaves, with striking, dark brownish-red transverse stripes, and a narrow, sword-shape raceme, 30-60 cm long, consisting of yellow flowers and overlapping, orangey-red or red bracts.

V. zamorensis has plain, pale green leaves, a branching flowerhead, a greenish-red stem and white flowers with bright red bracts with yellow tips.

This plant is usually purchased when the flowering stem has already developed, and dies after flowering. To ensure that it flowers for a long time,. place the plant in a light spot, protected from the sun (east or north-facing window). 18-20° C. Always keep the soil fairly moist. Water with tepid, lime-free water, also in the cup (except in winter, when it should be empty). In summer, add lime-free plant food once a month. Remove young shoots (carefully) from the parent plant when the roots have formed, and plant in lime-free soil, e.g., a mixture of peat, sphagnum moss, leaf-mould and old cow manure, in a light spot, protected from sunlight. Minimum, 18° C. Ensure high relative humidity, keep moderately moist and spray frequently with lime-free water. During the growing season (spring/summer), also water in the cup. In winter, water less (empty cup). After three years, the plant can be wrapped in a plastic bag with ripe apples (which secrete acetylene gas) and this will encourage it to flower after a few days. Repot if necessary in lime-free soil. Propagate from shoots and seed (this takes a long time).

Zantedeschia
Arum lily

⌓ ↕ 40-60 ◯ ✿ 2-5/5-7 ⊽ ◁

Zantedeschia, which is indigenous in South Africa, comprises about 8 species. It is a herbaceous marsh plant with thick, tuberous roots, fleshy stems, large, undivided, arrow-shaped, bright green leaves, and a striking bloom, consisting of a spadix with many florets, surrounded by a large, cup-shaped spathe.

Z. aethiopica (syn. *Richardia africana*), the Calla lily, has shiny green, wavy, heart-shaped leaves, and a yellow spadix with an ivory, trumpet-shaped spathe.

Z. elliottiana, yellow calla, has oval, heart-shaped leaves with white spots, and a stem, 60 cm long, with a golden-yellow spathe about 10 cm long, and a yellow spadix.

Z. rehmannii, pink calla, 40-60 cm tall, has narrower, oval, lanceolate leaves, with attractive silvery markings, and a narrow, pale or dark pink spathe and spadix, 8 cm long.

This plant requires a cool light spot protected from sunlight, and potting compost, rich in humus, mixed with clay and old cow manure. Keep moist at all times. Water and spray regularly, and feed once a week. 15° C. After flowering (September/October), it needs a resting period with no water. The leaves die off. Store the bulb in a dry, light, cool place for the winter. Repot in January, place in a warmer spot, water liberally and feed once a week. It can be placed in a moist spot in the garden, and be dug up in mid-October and stored in a cool place for the winter. Propagate by dividing the bulb and from seed.

Zantedeschia,
Arum lily

Summary

List of plant heights (in cm), flowering period, and flower colours. See the plant descriptions for further details.

	Height	Flowering period	Colours
Begonia	30-50	All year	Yellow, orange, red, pink, white
Browallia	30-75	All year	Blue, purple, white
Dendranthema	15-75	All year	Yellow, orange, purple, red, pink, white
Guzmania	40-75	All year	Yellow, orange to light red, yellowish-white, white
Kalanchoë	20-30	All year	Yellow, orange, purple, red, white
Neoregelia	25	All year	Lilac, purple, red
Primula	15-30	All year	Many different colours
Saintpaulia	10-20	All year	Blue, lilac, purple, pink, white, salmon
Senecio	20-30	All year	Blue, purplish-red, pink, terracotta, white
Triplochlamys	50-100	All year	Purple, pink, red
Citrofortunella	75-300	Repeat-flowering	Orange-yellow
Rosa	15-40	Repeat-flowering	Yellow, orange, red, pink, violet, white
Columnea	50-200	Varies	Yellow, orange, red
Rhododendron	30-50	Varies	Orange, red, pink, violet, white
Cyclamen	25-40	Sep-Mar	Red, pink, white
Ardisia	50-100	Sep-May	White, pink, red
Euphorbia	30-80	Oct-Jan	Cream, yellow, red, white
Calceolaria	25-50	Oct-May	Yellow, orange, red
Helleborus	15-30	Nov-Dec	White to pink, green
Hippeastrum	50-70	Nov-Apr	Red, pink, white, salmon, two-coloured
Hyacinthus	15-25	Nov-Apr	Blue, pink, white
Zantedeschia	40-60	Feb-May	Yellowish-white, pink
Medinilla	70-100	Feb-Aug	Pink
Spathiphyllum	30-70	Mar-Apr	Greenish-white, white
Jasminum	50-400	Mar-May	Yellow, white, whitish-pink
Nertera	5-15	Mar-May	Orange
Ardisia	50-100	Mar-Jun	White, pink, red
Hydrangea	50-100	Mar-Jun	Blue, red, pink, white
Brunfelsia	60	Mar-Aug	Blue, yellow, white
Pelargonium	25-80	Mar-Aug	Many different colours
Calathea	30-40	Mar-Sep	Orange-yellow
Hibiscus	30-100	Mar-Sep	Yellow, lilac, red, white, salmon, mixed
Passiflora	30-50	Mar-Sep	Bluish-white, lilac-white
Thunbergia	50-80	Mar-Sep	Blue, yellow, orange, white
Jathropha	60	Mar-Oct	Orange, red
Pachystachys	50-75	Mar-Oct	Yellow
Aphelandra	30-50	Apr-Aug	Yellow, orange, red
Clivia	30-60	Apr-Aug	Orange-red
Gomphrena	30-60	Apr-Aug	Orange, purple, red, pink, white, salmon
Sinningia	20-30	Apr-Aug	Purple, red, reddish-white, white
Beloperone	40-90	Apr-Sep	Brownish-red, green, salmon red
Clerodendrum	30-150	Apr-Sep	Pinkish-red, scarlet, white
Mandevilla	30-50	Apr-Sep	Purple, pink, white
Gloriosa	100-500	May-Jul	Orange-red/yellow
Zantedeschia	40-60	May-Jul	Yellowish-white, pink
Anigozanthos	50-150	May-Aug	Yellowish-green, reddish-brown
Billbergia	45-90	May-Aug	Pinkish-red, multicoloured
Impatiens	15-90	May-Aug	Orange, lilac, red, pink, white, two-coloured
Acalypha	50-75	May-Sep	Yellowish-white, purplish-red, red
Achimenes	15-60	May-Sep	Rred, pink, violet
Bougainvillea	30-50	May-Sep	Orange, purple, red, pink, white
Euphorbia	30-80	May-Sep	Cream, yellow, red, white
Eustoma	30-70	May-Sep	Purple, pink, white
Plumbago	30-50	May-Sep	Blue, pinkish-red, white
Aechmea	40-60	May-Oct	Orange/yellow, pink/blue, red
Aeschynanthus	50-300	May-Oct	Orange, red
Anthurium	30-60	May-Oct	Cream, orange, red, pink, white, salmon
Gloxinia	40-50	May-Oct	Orange-red
Streptocarpus	15-60	May-Oct	Blue, red, pink, white
Vriesea	30-190	May-Oct	Red, purple, yellow, white
Gardenia	60-150	Jun-Aug.	White
Celosia	15-60	Jun-Sep	Cream, yellow, orange, purple, red, pink

	Height	Flowering period	Colours
Duchesnea	20-25	Jun-Sep	Yellow
Gerbera	30-50	Jun-Sep	Cream, yellow, orange, red, pink, white
Justicia	50-100	Jun-Sep	Salmon pink to purplish-pink
Stephanotis	25-50	Jun-Sep	White
Cuphea	15-40	Jun-Oct	Red/white
Kohleria	20-60	Jul-Aug	Yellow, orange, red, pink, violet, white
Campanula	30	Jul-Sep	Blue, white
Hoya	30-50	Jul-Sep	Flesh-coloured/red, white/pinkish-red
Ixora	90-120	Jul-Sep	Yellow, orange, red, white
Exacum	20-35	Jul-Oct	Lilac-blue, lilac-pink, whitish-pink

Full sun, warm (16-20°C) (P) = protect from full sun

Acalypha (P)	Gerbera	Jasminum (P)	Pachystachys
Anigozanthos	Gomphrena	Jathropha	Pelargonium
Celosia (P)	Hibiscus (P)	Justicia (P)	Rosa
Gardenia (P)	Hippeastrum	Kalanchoë	Thunbergia

Full sun, moderately warm (10-16°C)

Bougainvillea	Gomphrena	Jasminum (P)	Passiflora
Citrofortunella	Hibiscus (P)	Kalanchoë	Pelargonium

Full sun, cool (3-10°C)

Cuphea (P)	Zantedeschia (P)

Full sun or semi-shade, moderate to warm

Beloperone	Euphorbia (P)	Hoya (P)	Mandevilla (P)
Billbergia (P)	Eustoma (P)	Hyacinthus	Triplochlamys
Campanula (P)	Gloriosa	Impatiens (P)	Vriesea (P)
Clerodendrum (P)			

Semi-shade, warm

Achimenes	Ardisia	Gloxinia	Medinilla
Aechmea	Columnea	Guzmania	Plumbago
Aeschynanthus	Duchesnea	Ixora	Sinningia
Aphelandra	Exacum	Kohleria	Stephanotis

Semi-shade, moderately warm

Ardisia	Calceolaria	Primula	Saintpaulia
Browallia	Cyclamen	Rhododendron	Streptocarpus
Brunfelsia	Plumbago		

Semi-shade, cool

Cyclamen	Helleborus	Neoregelia	Primula
Dendranthema	Hydrangea	Nertera	Rhododendron
			Senecio

Semi-shade or shade, moderate to warm

Anthurium	Begonia	Calathea	Clivia
			Spathiphyllum

Columnea gloriosa

Action:
– select clean, larger sized pot; line bottom of pot with crocks and a thin layer of fresh potting compost;
– tap sharply on the old pot and slide out the root ball; gently remove some of old compost with your fingers (taking care not to damage the roots) and place in the new pot;
– fill in with fresh compost to just above the old root ball, and firm the compost;
– keep the rim base free of compost to allow for watering.

Maintenance

Indoor plants will give you a great deal of pleasure if they are correctly positioned and suit the layout of the room. Given the right amount of light and the correct temperature, it is possible to have flowers in bloom for most of the year. If you do have a few weeks when there are no flowers in the house, you could always buy another plant to fill in the gap, but you will get more pleasure from well-chosen, long-lasting plants. Ultimately, their success will depend on how well you look after them.

You can achieve wonderful effects by placing plants at different heights: on windowsills, on the floor, and on tables and other raised surfaces. Rows of shelves full of plants are also very attractive visually. The sizes of the plants themselves will depend on the amount of space you have available: smaller plants usually look their best when grown in groups and on a raised surface so that you can see them easily.

All plants need a careful balance of light, humidity and temperature, as well as an appropriate period of daylight. They are also unlikely to flourish unless you use a suitable container kept filled with fresh potting compost and watered properly. Some plants are quite happy with limited daylight during winter; others may need artificial lighting of some kind. All plants need some light, but direct sunlight is usually too much of a good thing, and may cause leaf scorch.

Centrally heated rooms are often a problem because the air in them is not humid enough for the plants. This can be helped by regular spraying.

Some plants need a period of rest before they will flower, which means keeping them in a cool but frost-free place during winter, and reducing watering. Plants should normally be fed only during the growing season in spring and summer. Some need regular pinching out if they are to remain bushy and attractive.

Repotting

Normally, plants should be repotted once a year at the beginning of the growing season; larger plants need normally be repotted only once every two to three years, unless otherwise stated in the plant descriptions.

Potting on is necessary when
– the roots start to emerge through the bottom of the pot;
– lime scale appears on the clay pot;
– the plant begins to wither.

Many plants are quite happy with standard potting compost; here again, any exceptions are specified in the descriptions.

Always use clean pots when repotting, and place a layer of broken crocks at the bottom for drainage. Always handle the root ball very carefully. Press the compost firmly into the pot, leaving two to three centimetres at the top so that the water does not run off (see illustration).

Ordinary terracotta flowerpots are ideal, because they allow evaporation through the pot, though they are not always the most attractive containers for indoor plants and may need to be placed in ornamental pot holders. If you do not have drainage materials at the bottom of a pot, it should always have a hole to prevent surplus water from accumulating in the soil. Plastic pots are lightweight and easily stackable for storage purposes, but they do not allow evaporation through the sides and again may need to be placed in a plant pot holder.

Propagation

Generally speaking, houseplants are easy to propagate. This is probably one of the reasons why they are so popular.

The three main methods of propagation are division, cuttings and propagation by seed.

Cuttings are a particularly satisfying way of propagating many plants: these are taken during the growing season, usually in spring. Many plants, such as *Aeschynanthus*, *Hoya* and *Hydrangea*, are propagated from stem cuttings about 7 cm long; others, including *Kalanchoe*, *Saintpaulia* and *Streptocarpus*, are best grown from leaf cuttings. Dip the cuttings in hormone rooting powder and plant them in sandy soil (see illustration).

	Spring	Autumn	Winter/Dormant period
Repot	**	if necessary	
Take cuttings	**	*	
Feed	*		–
Little/no water			*

Buying hints

It is best to organize the arrangement of plants in the home in stages, in accordance with your design.
- First make a list of plants, also for friends who make gifts.
- Visit a number of suppliers on the basis of this list and test their expertise and range.
- There are nurseries and garden centres with a wide range of house plants. Buying all your plants from one place has advantages and disadvantages. It is a matter of confidence, expert advice and sympathy when dealing with complaints.
- Also look at the larger objects: plant table, rack, plant boxes, tubs or large pots (which fit in with the furniture).
- Make a choice from the enormous range of small pots in two or three sizes.
- A number of plants are available all year round. Some varieties flower several times or even all year round.
- Buy plants with a permanent clump, without moss or weeds. None of the roots should protrude (above or under the pot).
- Do not buy any plants which have bare branches or yellowing or brown leaves in the growing season.
- Cheap offers are often risky, but are sometimes very satisfactory.
- Mature plants in large pots are relatively expensive, but usually give value for money.
There is no guarantee of quality for ornamental plants. The occasional failure is to be expected by any plant enthusiast.
There are a hundred and one rules for looking after plants, good rules and bad rules, which actually stop a lot of people enjoying the uncomplicated pleasure of having plants in the home. You can always experiment. Remember that the plants are there for you, and not the other way round.

Pinching out
Pinching out helps to create fuller plants. Removing (by cutting or pinching out) the tip of a shoot will produce new shoots.

Propagation from cuttings
- *Take a 10-15 cm tip cutting with leaves and a bud from a young, non-flowering shoot.*
- *Remove the lower leaves.*
- *Dip the base of the cutting in hormone rooting powder.*
- *Insert the cutting in moist cutting compost.*
- *Press the compost down firmly and water.*

Small workers in the house

Life on house plants
The wealth of flowering plants in our homes has constantly increased in the last few years. However, with all these flowers and leaves an enormous world of tiny animals has also come into our homes.

Barn swallow,
Hirundo rustica

Many of these living creatures prey on the house plants which suddenly develop spots, sticky leaves, grey webs in the leaf axilla or round scales on the veins and stem. These scales are the most visible of all the harmful creatures; they are scale insects.

House fly,
Musca domestica

Scale insects
Normally developed larvae emerge from the eggs. The females adhere to a plant, lose their legs, eyes and antennae and then remain on the plant like a scale. Safely protected by the scale they remain in the same place all their life, feeding on the juices of the plant. This is also where they reproduce. The males are much more elongated and develop wings so that they start to look like mosquitoes. They live only to fertilize the females.
However, these are not the only scale insects which feed on house plants. There are also woolly aphids, which have a white woolly exterior, and ordinary scale insects.
All these undesirable guests secrete a sweet sticky substance which is known as honeydew, and not only serves as a nutrient for mould, but also irresistibly attracts flies.

Flies
Flies feel perfectly at home in the warm, even climate of our houses. In the first place, there are common house flies which follow people everywhere. Although many of us know that flies are dirty creatures, the real danger is often underestimated. They can transmit all sorts of diseases with their mouths because they eat what we eat. Therefore, it makes sense to be thankful for the spiders in our homes, which do more good than harm.

Spiders
Many people have a revulsion, and sometimes even a fear of spiders, although spiders are not harmful to anyone or anything. Like the common house fly, there is also a common house spider. They are bitter enemies. The house spider which lives with us, whether we like it or not, weaves horizontal webs in the corners of rooms or by windows, and catches all sorts of insects which we will prefer to lose. The almost microscopically small insects in flowerpots and window-boxes are not on the menu, however. It is only possible to get rid of these by regularly changing the soil.

Spider,
Tegenaria domestica

In fact, these small creatures don't do much harm, though they undeniably include some strange specimens. For example, a moist window box may be crawling with springtails. These are very primitive creatures which live on dead vegetable matter. They move along by hopping. As their name indicates, they hop with the help of their tail, which is curled under the body and which they use to push off with great force. They are amusing creatures and quite harmless to man.

Springtail,
Siphonaptera sp.

List of symbols

▪	annual
▪▪	biennial
○	perennial
◊	bulbous plant
◊	tuberous plant
⊥	tree
⊥	shrub
↕	height in cm
↔	interval between plants in cm
○	full sunlight
◐	semi-shade
●	shade
❀	flowering months
❋	winter-hardy
!	poisonous
✂	suitable for cut flowers
⚘	berry
🪣	keep moist at all times, compost should not dry out
🪣	keep moderately moist, compost may dry out slightly
🪣	keep fairly dry, only water during growing period
⊹	spray, avoid spraying when plant is flowering